PARALLAX

FARRAR STRAUS GIROUX

NEW YORK

SINÉAD MORRISSEY

★

PARALLAX

AND SELECTED POEMS

Farrar, Straus and Giroux

120 Broadway, New York 10271

Parallax originally published in 2013 by Carcanet Press, Great Britain

Published in the United States in 2015 by Farrar, Straus and Giroux

First American paperback edition, 2016

The Library of Congress has cataloged the hardcover edition as follows:

Morrissey, Sinéad, 1972–

[Poems. Selections]

Parallax : and selected poems / Sinéad Morrissey. —

First American edition.

pages ; cm

ISBN 978-0-86547-829-9 (hardcover) —

ISBN 978-0-374-71383-6 (ebook)

I. Title.

PR6063.07977 A6 2015

821'.914—dc23

2014043835

Paperback ISBN: 978-0-374-53613-8

Designed by Quemadura

www.fsgbooks.com

www.twitter.com/fsgbooks

www.facebook.com/fsgbooks

FOR JOSEPH

CONTENTS

From

THROUGH THE SQUARE WINDOW

(2009)

FROM

BETWEEN HERE AND THERE

(2002)

IN BELFAST

Here the seagulls stay in off the Lough all day.
Victoria Regina steering the ship of the City Hall
in this the first and last of her intense provinces,
a ballast of copper and gravitas.

The inhaling shop-fronts exhale the length
and breadth of Royal Avenue, pause,
inhale again. The city is making money
on a weather-mangled Tuesday.

While the house for the Transport Workers' Union
fights the weight of the sky and manages
to stay up, under the Albert Bridge the river
is simmering at low tide and sheeted with silt.

II

I have returned after ten years to a corner
and tell myself it is as real to sleep here
as the twenty other corners I have slept in.
More real, even, with this history's dent and fracture

splitting the atmosphere. And what I have been given
is a delicate unravelling of wishes
that leaves the future unspoken and the past
unencountered and unaccounted for.

This city weaves itself so intimately
it is hard to see, despite the tenacity of the river
and the iron sky; and in its downpour and its vapour I am
as much at home here as I will ever be.

AND FORGIVE US OUR TRESPASSES

Of which the first is love. The sad, unrepeatable fact
that the loves we shouldn't foster burrow faster and linger longer
than sanctioned kinds can. Loves that thrive on absence, on lack
of return, or worse, on harm, are unkillable, Father.
They do not die in us. And you know how we've tried.
Loves nursed, inexplicably, on thoughts of sex,
a return to touched places, a backwards glance, a sigh—
they come back like the tide. They are with us at the terminus
when cancer catches us. They have never been away.
Forgive us the people we love—their dragnet influence.
Those disallowed to us, those who frighten us, those who stay
on uninvited in our lives and every night revisit us.
Accept from us the inappropriate
by which our dreams and daily scenes stay separate.

Even though no one has died and there is no one
to touch in the coffin the way my brother
touched the dead-man relation
whose name we didn't know, whose features furrowed
like set sugar and whose black nails shone—
I have need of a funeral.

Even though death is not where I wish to go to,
down the wet green road through the strait black gate—
I have love in the morning, a candle, a radio
and a child's smile blooms over my fireplace.
If I don't walk to the river the river is by my window—
I have need of a funeral.

It came to me the day I stole communion in the cathedral,
not knowing what to do and squinting wildly,
that I had need of a funeral.
Something the man said as he tipped wine
and crushed bread felt helpful. He said sometimes a line
between what was and what is can be visible,

which is why we eat flesh and drink blood. *Kirie.*
I took flowers, an Oxfam veil, a bottle of Scotch, a speech
and made it to the sprawl of Milltown Cemetery
where I littered a hill with old shoes and milk teeth.

There was a pattern to the pattern my breath made on the air
as it extended towards the motorway.

These creatures live on faith that the greater sea,
whose roaring pounds and permeates the rock pool's floor,
the rock pool's leather-bound sanctuary, will once again rise up
to the little sea and that their salts will mingle and hold.
My arm submerged is a Eucalyptus tree
in an eighteenth-century birthing room, lurid and luminous.

How the women who have blocked the keyholes
and the door jambs with rags and snuffed the candles scurry!
They move as suddenly as the travelling specks of eyes
that haunt vision: one look at them and they're gone
but they still look on. Water pours from the raised fringe
of green gauze like generosity. The pool collects itself again.

These creatures have lodged themselves on the tallest ridge
of the law of averages, the law of probability, and on the memory
of what their ancestors learned and saw, as unswayably
as they swell in crevices and suck rocks. Life flourishes on
    belief—
it announces quietly how, some day or night, the sea will arrive
    and save them
from the starfish-seeking children and evaporation.

How they would shine in a parable on the return of Christ.

How they would give women succour, those who also hang on

for the moon to peak and for water to answer. A stick breaks but
    does not break

as it enters the mirror. When I bend to the surface the room
    underwater

clouds and furrows with breath like a door closing over.

I am not theirs and they will not give me up.

STITCHES

There has been extravagance in speech
and every spilled, exploded word has been a stitch
in a blanket made for an imaginary baby.
The words went south where the sun was, but stayed hungry.

A name came in the third month. A face followed.
A hair type, a footprint, but the stitches showed.
Imagination's cloth too coarsely woven
for life to catch and cover stitching over.

And then blood. Inevitable, true.
Simple and strong enough to cut all falsehood through.
Later the screen said darkness—no spine, no heart.
And the stitches came apart.

JO GRAVIS IN HIS METAL GARDEN

From the window of the midnight-bound Vegas plane
Tucson flares in the desert—a cactus pricked by rain;
lit houses, lit highways and floodlit swimming pools—
a stunned bird in a basin, spreading its wings to cool.
The gaudiness of Winterhaven is visible from air
in the aftermath of Christmas. Down in the dazzle somewhere
Jo Gravis is sleeping in his metal garden. It took a year
of free time strung like stepping stones from hour to hour
to finally clear his yard of rocks and the herbs he grew
as a solitary failed commercial venture—ginseng and feverfew.
Each hour of work an island. As though delivering his heart
from alcohol, he struck down to the bedrock of a humble start
and stood there a long time, exposed and rarified. At first,
he simply let the pictures come, withstood the thirst
and suffered the parade of soldiers, beggars, widows, orphans,
owls without trees and waterless swans and dolphins
until a gate latched in his mind and he had them forever.
He knew then he could commit them to metal to challenge the weather
and started to build. Metal the medium and metal the message,
he turned trolleys into children, knives into rose petals
from the pockets of Juan Diego, miraculous, crimson,
a velvet gift of proof from a virgin in a vision
hardened against the sun. He peeled flesh back from the bone
and fooled no one. When his women with aerial hair were done

his kettle-headed men stood guard against them by a river
of headlights and bicycle wheels. Such honesty in silver
puts constancy in a peeled hand of wires against the sky
and hope in a speechless sort of prophecy—
a teddy bear bound with twine to an orange tree,
its eyes replaced with pearls. With all of these images
hard and permanent and real and safe in cages
Jo Gravis sensed a sweet deliverance, an end to motion,
and finally built himself a wooden bench to sleep on
surrounded by signs—their shadows on his skin a lullaby
to flesh in a fleshless gallery.

My husband requests a sky burial
he wishes to be
as carrion sequestered by leopards
strung up in a desert tree

Back to the familiar corridor he
may choose any opening
but all the rooms contain me
dressed for a wedding

It is the easiest part of the day—the ending of it,
here, with you, among sheets that smell of our skin.
I would know your skin in the dark: its smooth magnetic film
would bring me home and cease my being separate
with one blind touch. I know it again now, this expanse
of noise and light between us. It conquers distance.

Hallways of childhood friends had smells, family smells
that followed family members into schools as stowaways
in coat sleeves and lunch boxes—slipped giveaways
of origin, of who made who, of what was left to tell
made suddenly clear in every detail as if recently rained on.
One was made of wine; one walked crushed by blankets even
    under sun;

one carried the antiseptic of insulin packets and coconut dust
about her, in her hair, and later what I knew by force
to be the thin, hard odour of divorce—
shipyard metal caving under sparks, spit, boot polish and rust.
And I knew also that whatever was in my hallway
was exposing the line and the set of my spine like an X-ray.

Now we too have an identity—
the smell of us is through our sheets and wrapped around our
    home—
invisible ink encoded onto bone.
We have wrought it as surely as any family
forges something wholly themselves and wholly different
and marks each child for life with the hidden nature of their
    generative act.

From you, the smell of the Tucson desert:
copper deposits, animal skulls, the chalk trajectory
of stars no cloud covers or stains, ochre and chilli.
From me, bog cotton, coal fires, wild garlic, river dirt.
And from the two of us, salt. When we move house
such genealogies as these will follow us.

ON WAITAKERE DAM

FOR CHARLES BROWN

You wanted to up-end the boat
and set it on the lake we lived by
because no one would know.
It was lavish with silverfish and looked
defeated, humped on its secret
like a hand. There was nowhere to go to

but the magnet of the middle lake
where a vapour sat wide as Australia—
as sovereign, as separate, as intimate
with daylight, as ignorant
of clocks and raincoats and boats.
It threw a soft, unwatchable shimmer

we would not be human in.
You dismantled a sky
as you tipped the boat over,
the nest of a possum was robbed.
The hull settled outside-in
as you inverted the universe.

We bobbed in the reeds.
The trees lay down their crowns
beneath us, an underwater canvas
of spectacular women. Above us
the crowds of their branches were cold.
Black swans were nesting in the nesting place,

trees reared to the rim of vision—
we slid on to the centre. At night,
with no lights for miles, the lake
would glitter with the Southern Cross.
It smiled at us
with a million silver teeth.

We'd heard it roar with rain
and watched it coughing eels
over the dam's brim,
too water-sore to keep them any longer.
They fell flinching themselves
into s's or n's.

And now we sat stilled in a boat
in the centre, under the lake's shroud,
and the listening
was for the car of the caretaker—
weaving down from the Nihotipu Dam
with Handel or Bach on the radio.

The black fish under the bridge was so long I mistook it
for a goldfish in a Japanese garden the kind the philosophers
wanted about them so much gold underwater to tell them what
    waited
in another element like breathing water they wanted to go
to the place where closing eyes is to see

I understood the day I closed my eyes in Gifu City I saw Japan
for the first time saw what I had seen the gate to the Nangu
Shrine by the Shinkansen stood straddled before my head and I
held out my hands to touch it and felt changed air it wasn't
there but I walked into it continually and over the gardens full
of pumpkin seeds in the ground and wild red flowers over them
    they told me

they brought autumn and they were about my head also in Gifu
    City all pearled
in mist and happy as Japanese brides. I saw the JR crates on the
    night
trains that passed through stations and seemed endless and
    running
on purpose on time's heels on sheer will to cross Honshu one end
to the other money's own messenger fire down the line. And
    when you talked me through

Gifu one end to the other eyes closed I saw what I would never
have seen sighted a transvestite taxi driver set apart on the street
a lost person flowers by the pavement pavements for the blind I
    saw
music as pulled elastic bands drums as the footprints of exacting
    gods

I mistook the black fish for an oriental goldfish the flash of gold
on its belly meant it carried its message for the element below it
always one storey down Zen masters attaining one storey down
    and I,
falling into you, story by story, coming to rest in the place where
    closing eyes is to see

No one seems sure of the reason why aprons
are tied to the necks of stone babies in temples.
The priest says 'honour'.
The guide to Kyoto City mentions 'cold
on their journey away from us to the heaven for children'.
I look at them squatting in Buddha-reflection,
wrapped up to the throat in teddy bears and trains.

★

There's a graveyard for miscarriages under Ikeda Mountain
as stark as a bone field. No flowers, tangerines, sake or aprons
but a basin of stone bodies in two parts: square body, round head.
Like oriental soldiers contained by a wall, they would go walking—
spill over with all of the energy for life that fell out of them too soon.
Except that even in stone some bodies have opened—
loose balls in the basin where heads have rolled.

★

Inside the biggest wooden building in the world
sits Japan's greatest Buddha. One hand raised as a stop sign to evil.
The other is flat, flat with comfort and promise, flat enough
for all of us to nuzzle his thumb. His lily flower opened.
His crossing was a falling into light.
Fall with me, he says, *and you'll be raised to the heights
of the roof of the biggest wooden building in the world.*

★

When Nagasawa visits the house of the dead
he leaves at the door his camera and tripod
his champion karaoke voice his miracle foot massage
his classroom dynamics his rock-hard atheism
and slips onto the tatami of the prayer room
as the man who can chant any you-name-it soul
between here and Ogaki to paradise.

SPRING FESTIVAL

My body has become the body of the festival:
the vaginas on shrines reduce me to the facts of life.
And my wedding vows to you are this festival's promises—

a roaring in the ears, narrow entrances,
and the two of us hauled into life's own procession
of mother after mother after mother.

SUMMER FESTIVAL

What do you think when you see a mâché vagina
being rammed with a penis as broad as a battering ram
so that children disguised as elements shriek with joy?

You think: *We are disembodied, while the moon herself has a body.*
She is over by the beer stands disguised as a man. One stagger and
    she'll trigger
the collapse of the dancers. The moon came to watch us and we all
    fell down.

AUTUMN FESTIVAL

The fields have been sealed with fire. They are singing
the promise of resurrection and revenge. The whole *cho*
scraped of rice and fruit, it is time to go under and store.

In the streets I watch women who are dancing in rings
in the slow, hindered steps of the kimono. Again and again,
a festival of women. They are declaring what's been done.

WINTER FESTIVAL

They'll padlock themselves with sake against the cold.
They'll bandage their loins. They'll straddle a drum on its side
made from pulled skin and the sign of an upright swastika

and they'll move on a sea of bare men's shoulders, tall as trees,
banging only when the silence has become unendurable.
In the alley there's a pyramid of bright flesh and lanterns,
    refusing to be born.

Too far back to imagine
It was all dissolved
Under soft black strokes
Of a Chinese brush
Diminishing the fatness
Of original things

Animal legs and human legs are emptied of flesh and blood

Patterns from flattened
Ants or a lake drained the facts
That are trees in winter
The spokes of the world went down
In a language that
Went everywhere, stayed put

Put out what you want a woman and man to be the picture will
   hold that too

There are stories in skeletons
And after the three fluid
Lines that are Mountain, the four
That are Fire, Ice as a stroke
On the left side of Water—
Problem is Tree in a Box

I hear moaning and see constriction in a picture the colour is
　　cinnamon the taste is chalk

A mind is inside the lines
All of it and sooner or later
Sex is everywhere, money
Rice fields wives are mostly
Under the roof to like
Is Woman with Child

I get lost in a landscape of noisy ideas that cross and flare in the
　　fireworks of strokes

Like a child who paints a smile
Over signatures makes Yin
And Yang (two kissing fish)
A rising sun in a field
Of wheat I draw windows leaking
On the kanji for Rain

I make my moon round my forest has branches my people are
　　walking with arms and a head

And then murder comes, a second

Killing, so softly I'm deaf

At the second of entrance.

My pictures defy the eyes.

I see Lamentation as five falling stars,

Grief abroad and walking,

And a terrible stag, flames shooting from his heart, as he prepares
to walk and preach.

THE STATE OF THE PRISONS

FLIGHT

There he saw one *Anne Bridlestone* drove through the streets by an
officer of the same corporation, holding a rope in his hand, the other
end fastened to an engine called the branks, which is like a crown,
it being of iron, which was musled over the head and face, with a great
gag or tongue of iron forced into her mouth, which forced the blood out;
and that is the punishment which the magistrates do inflict upon chiding
and scoulding women; and he hath often seen the like done to others.

—*England's Grievance Discovered* (1655)

After the murder of our blessèd Martyr,
After the slaughter of the rout at Worcester,
His son the rightful king went into hiding—
Here as a woodcutter, there as a serving-man—
Disguising the telltale milk-white of His skin
By the dye of rotted walnuts. 1651:
The Year of Our Lord that my husband bridled me
And I have learned to hold my tongue in company.

*

He could not remain unrecognised for long,
Majesty being so natural unto Him,
It soon shone forth. But was He loved!
He walked upon the bones of England,

Sought solace at farms and hid in the crowns of trees
And all of nature shadowed Him. His enemies
Sifted the land and still His face was not revealed.
It is my love of Him bleeds when I speak out loud.

★

He has stood in a fall of rain
While Cromwell's men sang psalms against Him
And did not venture in. He has seen women
Sink to their knees and then raise their hand in blessing.
My husband desires a sign.
But for all his reading of *Revelation*
I say heaven admits its own
And it is Him. The jaw-straps tighten.

★

The changeling Prince vanished to France.
Deadwinter dismembers us.
Christmas consumes its own bright fire
And blazes by its absence. There is too much law
To live by, and I have torn my face
In two by swallowing silence.
My husband leads me through the marketplace
As the village women gape.

GENETICS

My father's in my fingers, but my mother's in my palms.
I lift them up and look at them with pleasure—
I know my parents made me by my hands.

They may have been repelled to separate lands,
to separate hemispheres, may sleep with other lovers,
but in me they touch where fingers link to palms.

With nothing left of their togetherness but friends
who quarry for their image by a river,
at least I know their marriage by my hands.

I shape a chapel where a steeple stands.
And when I turn it over,
my father's by my fingers, my mother's by my palms

demure before a priest reciting psalms.
My body is their marriage register.
I re-enact their wedding with my hands.

So take me with you, take up the skin's demands
for mirroring in bodies of the future.
I'll bequeath my fingers, if you bequeath your palms.
We know our parents make us by our hands.

It was black as the slick-stunned coast of Kuwait
over Belfast Lough when the whales came up
(bar the eyelights of aeroplanes, angling in into the airport
out of the east, like Venus on a kite string being reeled
to earth). All night they surfaced and swam
among the detritus of Sellafield and the panic
of godwits and redshanks.

By morning
we'd counted fifty (species *Globicephala melaena*)
and Radio Ulster was construing a history. They'd left a sister
rotting on a Cornish beach, and then come here, to this dim
smoke-throated cistern, where the emptying tide leaves a scum
of mussel shell and the smell of landfill and drains.
To mourn? Or to warn? Day drummed its thumbs
on their globular foreheads.

Neither due,
nor quarry, nor necessary, nor asked for, nor understood
upon arrival—what did we reckon to dress them in?
Nothing would fit. Not the man in oilskin working in the warehouse
of a whale, from the film of Sir Shackleton's blasted *Endeavour*,
as though a hill had opened onto fairytale measures
of blubber and baleen, and this was the money-
god's recompense;

                               not the huge Blue

seen from the sky, its own floating eco-system, furred
at the edges with surf; nor the unbridgeable flick
of its three-storey tail, bidding goodbye to this angular world
before barrelling under. We remembered a kind of singing,
or rather our take on it: some dismal chorus of want and wistfulness
resounding around the planet, alarmed and prophetic,
with all the foresight we lack—

                              though not one of us

heard it from where we stood on the beaches and car-parks
and cycle-tracks skirting the water. What had they come for?
From Carrickfergus to Helen's Bay, birdwatchers with binoculars
held sway while the city sat empty. The whales grew frenzied.
Children sighed when they dived, then clapped as they rose
again, Christ-like and shining, from the sea, though they could
    have been
dying out there,

                           smack bang

in the middle of the ferries' trajectory, for all we knew.
Or attempting to die. These were Newfoundland whales,
radically adrift from their feeding grounds, but we took them
as a gift: as if our own lost magnificent ship
had re-entered the Lough, transformed and triumphant,
to visit us. As if those runaway fires on the spines of the hills
had been somehow extinguished . . .

For now,

they were here. And there was nothing whatsoever to be said.

New islands in the water between Eden and Holywood.

CHINA

2

A tunnel of trees. My brother and I on the top
of an empty double-decker in Derbyshire.
The absence-from-home of summer
becoming a scab to be picked over. The bus pulled up

by a pub, as the greenery scratching
at the window ended and we were given a field
with a horse and a dog and a red child
in it, waving.

Sunlight was there like a wall
and halved everything. In my head I was singing
This is Happening This is Happening This is Happening.
A boy bounced his way down the aisle

and started smoking, when time
opened. Or stopped. Or almost stalled
and the boy and my brother and the bus and the world
disappeared on the prick of a needle—pop!—and I

sat sideways avoiding the gap.
And then I saw I was enormous
and in another kind of tunnel. That I was lost.
That there was no going back.

3

Conjure the Yangtze and the Yellow River
And bring them a matter of hours together
On the same train line and both of them seen
Through semi-darkness on a flickering screen
Which is and is not a window. Blow
Over the waters to buckle them. Add snow.

5

Evening. Beijing. And farwell to Mao's mausoleum
through the glass, ablaze in the nerves of the Square of Heaven
like everlasting Christmas. The bus forces us on:
another station, another train, another city, another season.
Advertising flickers in the waiting room. That night I dive like a
    child—
borne aloft by the train's engine, or like one born again in its mild
motion, the shunt and click of the carriages over the sidings
the soporific tenderness of a language I do not recognise—
and re-surface at nine, an hour beyond breakfast time.
The mine wheels, factories, fish farms, and allotments
battling for space between slack-blackened tenements
have receded now into the north. Here the sky is unfolding the blue
cloth of itself on a new country, or on a country which never grew
old to begin with. Spinach, pak choi, cabbage greens, lettuce,

geese sunning themselves among shiny brown cowls of the lotus
and an echo-less emptiness, a sense of perspective too wide
and too high for the eye to take in. Two crows collide
in a rice field, then are flung backwards out of their war
as the train pushes on. We loiter like Oliver in the dining car.
Brunch comes as simmering bowls of noodles, under a film
of oil, and we sit watching the landscape unfurl like a newsreel
into history. By noon, foothills are banking to the south.
By two, we're approaching a network of tunnels blasted out
of the Xi'an Qin Mountains. Blackness falls clean as a guillotine
on the children in pairs by the trackside, and then again
on the man and his son who will walk all afternoon into evening
before they are home. We enter Sichuan without rupturing
any visible line of division, though dinner at five is brimming
    with chillies:
dried and diced and fried with the seeds inside, while the
    extraordinary
Sichuan pepper balloons into flavour under our tongues. And
    all along
darkness is gathering itself in. I see a boy and a woman
lit up by the flare of a crop fire, but can no longer believe in them.
Windows have turned into mirrors the length of the train.
Hours pass, and there is only my white face, strained
in its hopelessness, my failure to catch the day in my hands like
    a fish
and have it always. The train descends from the soil terraces.
Electricity switches the world back on: town after coal-dusted town

streams by in the rain, revealing its backdoor self, its backyard
    frown,
until all converge in a Day-Glo glare at the end of the line and we
    merge
with our destination. We have been dropped to the bottom of
    somewhere
blurred and industrial, where the yellow of the Yangtze meets the
    green
of its tributary, the city with a name like the din of a smithy:
    Chongqing.

7

I find I have made a ghost
of you—I'm sorry—as I
aimed my camera foolishly
at the passing coloratura
of mountains and fields,
and snapped them anyway,
knowing I'd never get them back
the way they were being given,
at that precise instant, and caught them,
yes all right, adequately enough, but somehow
also caught your watchful face
filling the window without
its source. Confucius refuses
to speak about spirits. *Till you know*

about the living, how are you
to know about the dead? he pronounces
to the ever-curious Tzu-lu.
And I wonder, if I can make ghosts
of the living with my dinky, digital
machine, is it possible I can also
make the dead visible? And I set my camera
more deliberately now on the vast peopleless
expanse, then check its screen
to see if I've got anything
in its wide-eyed little net.
I don't know what I expected—
one or two of the million Yangtze
drowned, perhaps, still draining their ears
by banging the sides of their heads, or looking after
the vanishing tumult of the train
for directions home?

9

One day, China met China in the marketplace.
'How are you, China?' asked China, 'we haven't talked in so long.'
China answered: 'The things we have to say to one another,
          laid end to end, and side to side,
would connect the Great Wall with the Three Gorges Valley
          and stretch nine miles up towards the sun.'
'It's true,' replied China. 'We have a lot to catch up on.'

Is it for their failures that I love them?
Ignoring the regulation of *Selected Poems*,
with everything in that should be in—
all belted & buttoned & shining—
I opt instead for omnivorous *Completes*.
For their froth. Their spite. For avoidable mistakes:
Larkin on Empire, say, or Plath on Aunts.

The thrill of when they dip, trip up, run out
of things to write about before they start,
is the consolation of watching
a seascape suddenly drained and stinking
of flies & fisheads & bladderwrack.
And the tide impossibly distant. And no way back.
Yes, I love them for that.

CLOCKS

The sadness of their house is hard to defeat. There are at least
   three clocks per room.
There are two people with nothing to do but to be in each room
   and be separate.
The person each room was decorated by was seconded to a plot
   in a cemetery
that is walked to every day, and tended like a bedroom sanctuary.
   No notice given.
The clocks do all the talking. He visits the grave in the middle of
   a three-hour loop
and knows the year of completion of every castle in Ireland. His
   route
is always the same: the round tower via the aqueduct via the
   cemetery via the ramparts
via the Battle of Antrim during the Rising of the United Irishmen
   in 1798,
the slaughter of which is more present if he's deep in the morning
of his April wedding breakfast or locked into the moment they
   fitted the oxygen mask
and she rolled her bruised eyes back. She is unable to find the
   stop for the bus to Belfast
and stays indoors. The nets turn the daylight white and empty.
She has worn the married life of her sister so tightly

over her own, the noise of the clocks makes her feel almost without
   skin.

Sometimes she sits in her sister's chair, and feels guilty.
She has *Countdown* for company and a selective memory—
the argument at the funeral with her niece over jewellery and,
   years ago,
the conspiracy to keep her single, its success. Time settles over
   each afternoon
like an enormous wing, when the flurry of lunchtime has left them
and the plates have already been set for tea. He reads extensively—
from *Hitler and Stalin: Parallel Lives* to *Why Ireland Starved*—
but has taken to giving books away recently to anyone who calls.
Winter or summer, evenings end early: they retire to their separate
   rooms
at least two hours before sleep. It falls like an act of mercy
when the twenty-two clocks chime eight o'clock in almost perfect
   unison.

THE YELLOW EMPEROR'S CLASSIC

AFTER GONG SUN

The body is China.
Middle Kingdom between here
and hereafter, it is compromised from the start.
Messengers are important.

China has been an imperial system
for centuries, and repeats itself endlessly.
The heart is its Emperor.
All other organs are the Emperor's courtiers—

see poor pericardium
go slack with deflected shame.
A king may never be blamed directly, so
heart-sac swallows heart-blows uncomplainingly.

We are constantly at the mercy
of pernicious influences: cold, damp, dry, wind,
heat and summer heat. (There are two kinds
of summer in the Chinese calendar.)

These are also known as the six evils.
When the spirit exits, it exits
from the back of the neck. The body
opens and shuts itself to damage

like a gate refusing to be latched.
We muster control
of our orifices.
We fight back.

Sexual energy resides in the kidney,
lowest of all Yin organs
and root of the body tree.
Desire is pre-heaven essence.

It flows before birth,
bestowed wherever our souls
are stowed, in a limited vial
and fatally expendable.

There is a highway
of sexual awakening,
a road rather than a river
in spite of water.

At puberty a dignitary
(from heaven, ultimately)
slashes with his sword the blood-
silk ribbon and cries 'Open!'

Old Liver General
must ensure all *qi* troops
now pass
in an orderly fashion.

For there must be sex. True, too much
depletes our pre-heaven essence
and can result in weaknesses
of the lower trunk. But too little is catastrophic.

Like trying to survive
without our opposite
inside us
when opposites equal life.

China is haunted by celibate women
at risk from surfeit of Yin. Listen.
Withering from within, they are homesick
and wandering. Vengeful as ghosts.

Whatever else it was he stole from the East—
indigo, gold, a brace of abused and temporary women,
frankincense, the inevitable spice or two,
or the fruit that shed itself with such feral sweetness
on the tongue it begged re-naming—
Alexander also stowed nothing—
that double nick in the Babylonian plaque which,
of everything, was the easiest to store
(the women were a nightmare)
precisely because it lived nowhere
and therefore everywhere: in two spare horseshoes
angled together, in the kiss of a thumb and forefinger,
in the sigh at the bottom of a poured-out water jar,
in the memory of some noon-white city square
wherever luck ran out, or faith, or anger—

                                        but

when Alexander delivered zero to the Greeks
they turned and saw (or thought they saw)
a wellhead blacken in front of them—
an incredulous, bricked-in O—
unravelling into inkiness like a sleeve, the kind
you might toss a stone into and never hear the splash,
though you stand and wait, your ear awash in silence,
for an hour—and over it the bric-a-brac of kitchens appeared

suspended in the sunshine—knives, lemons, sieves, pots, bowls—
a funnel of dailyness, which the wellhead then swallowed
like a child, and, sensing where it could lead,
this number/no-number that would eat the world,
the Greeks turned back to Alexander in the advancing shade
and smiled: for there were still angles, there were still
three old angels skipping over heaven carrying harps and signs.

When Cathy came to New Zealand, my stepfather Charles
put on his woollen vest and Swan overcoat and peaked cap
with a rainbow embroidered on it and took us to see the waterfall.

He was a bushman: had grown up in the bush Up North
before ever there was a town the way Whangarei is a town today
with its flat whites and yellow taxicabs and Maori women drivers.
    Yes,

had shouldered his way into adulthood, into being army-wed,
from the bed of an eel-breeding creek, on the back of a Kauri trunk,
against the hard flat palm of a forest that—decades afterwards—

had still not been felled. So he knew where to take us and how to
    take us,
that winter afternoon, in the handclapping rain of the Waitakeres,
donning that pack of his as though he were back in Vietnam,

where all his booming dreams still happen, his casual jockey saunter
a bowsprit through the leaves, though he knew exactly what we
    might find
and wasn't daunted. And yet how tenderly they would park their
    cars—

some even bothering to hood the steering wheel in chains—
in viewing spots anywhere along the Scenic Drive, before breaking
    off
into the trees, when he would get the call to go and find them.

He'd cut them down after days sometimes. The branches of
    pongas
unfisted beside the railway line and the birds were indefatigable.
The rain was bringing the dark on early but you could still see

the entire steaming basin of greenery swallowing water
on your left side (my mother in her innocence asking,
the day she arrived from Ireland, *But who planted all this?*)

and Cathy and Joseph and Charles and I were increasingly more
    like
forked poles in a river than people as we came up to the mouth
of the train tunnel and waded inside. He could woo wood pigeons

just by talking to them and once one had rested on his hand.
Away from the thwack and clatter of the downpour and where
entrance and exit were two equidistant reminders of daylight

lived the glow-worms he spoke of, that were not worms at all
but a little boy's peel-and-stick galaxy, a lace of green needlepoint,
winking on after lights-out over the bunk bed. Out at the other end

and evening was gathering pace in the forest far faster than we'd
    predicted,
returning each towering layer of flax to one vast, dripping canopy.
By the rudiments of a siding shed—a rejected Korean asylum
    seeker

had survived here for a fortnight on trapped possums and stream
    water—
we angled ourselves for the climb and veered right, up through the
    breathing
trees, and what dusk there was had swung shut on a solitariness

of moss and lichen and spider orchids. Charles cut the way out in
    front of us
without slowing, insisting we still had time, his mind—who
    knows—
on the nights he'd lain down on the floor of a Singapore jungle,

with only a net to shelter in, and the insects in the air had shrieked
so accusingly at every rigid angle of his body, he couldn't sleep.
It had been raining now for a week. The Waitakere Dam was full—

even from here we could hear it batter itself over the brim
and the waterfall was the same: choked and slick and incandescent
in the dim cave it had made for itself. Our breaths came hard

and alien in the clearing as we took its kiss on our skin.
Charles stood like a conquistador, hand on one hip, looking up.
But already I was imagining the journey back, down through the
    slithering

dark, all three of us steady in his flashlight's wake, hitting the
    railway track
and then on through the tunnel and then up to the steps by the
    concrete expanse
of the dam face, and into the house near the watercress bank
    where my life

had been riveted for months. Our homecoming chorus the hunger
of owls, fierce and unassuageable—*morpork! morpork!*—
and Charles cocking his head at the sound of them as though they
    could speak.

THE STATE OF THE PRISONS

A HISTORY OF JOHN HOWARD,

PRISON REFORMER, 1726–1790

As for me, I will behold thy face in righteousness:
I shall be satisfied when I awake, with thy likeness.

—Psalm 17:15

I

I am a stranger and a pilgrim here.
I burn my letters, decline a monument, take heart
From the body's incontinence. The spirit departs.
The field hospitals of Russia with their horrendous dead
Must carry me home to the Lord my Maker
Where all my fathers' fathers stand assembled.

I see these soldiers' faces when I sleep.
And then they cloud and clear again as the child's
Who stopped me on the road to ask the time
And tried to steal my watch. How sick she is.
And then she splits, becomes three women beating hemp
In a bridewell, missing eyelids . . .

Death has no terrors for me.
I have ridden the Devil's coach road, I have discovered
It leads, in every city in Europe, to the mansions of governors.
Powders fizz in a glass. The admiral who has travelled
Thirty miles to smile encouragingly
Tries to change the subject but his voice unravels.

Death sits in my frame. And death shall have dominion
Where all bodies are. 70,000 Russian soldiers died the year before
I washed up on the far shore of the Crimea.
This figure summoned me to Stepanovka—
A detour from my quest to find the origin
Of plague. Now all such quests are over.

There is a village where a river flows
Through a grove of pine trees. It is peaceful and obscure,
Called Dauphigny. A Frenchman I befriended came from there.
We passed it on our journey south.
Bury me here in my chapel clothes
And let my body face the river mouth.

Fame saddens heaven. Suffer no stone to be raised to me,
Nor details of my life and works be given at the gravebed,
Nor mourners come. Erect a sundial over my head
Instead of an inscription. Read from the Psalms
Of beholding His face in righteousness. Forget me. To posterity,
I leave a syphilitic son, and a vision of prisons.

God sent an earthquake when I was twenty-nine
And lured my soul to suffering like moths to the flame.
November 1755. As my first wife was lain
In an oak box in Whitechapel, 20,000 attested dead
Flared across the pages of the *Gentleman's Magazine*.
The death toll left me breathless, but decided.

Resolved for Portugal, I dismissed my servants,
Sorted my affairs, and was heading for the wreckage on the Lisbon
    packet
On the 14th day in January, when the French attacked.
We were captured as prisoners of war, whipped,
And forced on our knees to swear a blood-felt testament
To dungeon existence. Later we were shipped

To Carhaix, then finally released. I came home.
Washed. Grew well. In time became Sheriff of Bedford.
The villagers and tenants prospered.
My French adventure faded from view. And then the County Trials,
Irregular as women, rolled round again to Cardington,
And everything changed. At the first sitting of the Assizes

The prisoners entered, pulling on long chains.
A muscle jerked in my thumb. The judge was eminent,
Bored, ecclesiastical, inured to the stench of sweat and excrement

That flowered where they stood. I was reeling back to a stone hole
And darkness interminable, as the felons' crimes
Were pronounced against them in a nasaloid drone.

When it was over, I barked six questions at the Crown officials.
Why are they not clean? Why so thin?
Why ill? Why are felons and debtors, women and men,
Chained and tried together? Why, when chosen for release,
Do debtors stay listed on the turnkey's roll call?
What fees remain to pay? Justice sat asleep

In a rolled wig. I metamorphosed into an enthusiast.
And so it was my journey started to every prison in Europe,
Shuttling between nations like an evangelist. Or *a Cook
Of the Unfortunate* (as Burke put it). I, too, was on a voyage of
    discovery.
I, too, would make maps. A continent of misery, uncharted, vast
Opened before my eyes. I vowed to regulate the colony.

3

Lord, keep me solitary to do Thy will.
My second wife, delivered of our only son
In 1765, afterwards died of a womb infection.
I was not designed for intimacy. The boy bothered me,
Mooning in my shadow like a criminal.
And sickly. I tried Lockean discipline: cold baths, daily;

Wet socks; no sweetmeats. He promised to obey me,

Even irrationally. I sat him in the root house once in February

And didn't lock the door, to see if he would stay

Despite the cold. (He stayed.) He was sent away to school, and
    manhood,

When he was four years old. Unshackled, free,

At lodgings in the capital, I joined the Kingdom of the Wicked.

Ah London! Thou vast ship of distress!

With Newgate at thy helm, ferrying the damned to Tyburn.

How many more were cut down by contagion?

The turnkey looked astounded when I asked to descend

To the felons' wards, armed with a notebook, and an
    all-but-useless

Phial of vinegar. Gaol fever, the pox, the flux, the pestilence

Raged down there. Later they claimed I was cloaked in
    righteousness—

I ascribe my immunity to God's Purpose and shallow breathing.

Even after riots in 1780 left Old Newgate smouldering,

They rebuilt the bastion with its heart intact.

I see it as I first entered it: putrid with grime, lice

Crunching underfoot, prostitutes parading in their Sunday hats.

I extended my research, living mostly on the road,

Eating and sleeping between prisons. My carriage stank

Obnoxiously in summer, so I switched to horseback.

Ipswich has no fireplace, Ely no straw, in Durham six prisoners
Were chained to the floor of a dungeon under a courtyard,
Up to their ankles in sewer water.

Like Luther, I made a list of grievances.
They say in hell the damned are separated, each to their own
    offence.
I saw both sexes sprawl like dogs in the marketplace
Through most of the prisons in England, the debtor drink gin with
    the highwayman,
The youthful and the innocent confined without allowances
For innocence or youth. I steadied myself for a reformation.

4

They said I rode like a horseman of the Apocalypse.
My circuit broadened: to Scotland, to Ireland, to the Continent.
It intensified: I saw schools, workhouses, hospitals for the indigent,
Asylums for the insane. I saw those confined by quarantine
As well as by crime. In truth, each journey was slow and
    treacherous:
60,000 miles of stony road, potholes, ditches and slime

Stretch between Dublin and Constantinople. And I remember
    them all.
I was travelling now obsessively.

The boy spent school holidays at Cardington without me.
My servant sent reports. *There are problems, Sir,*
Wrote Thomasson, warily, almost daring to be vocal,
Problems of a certain delicate nature—. Ignorance was my error.

Fame was busy, ever preceding me. I was never alone
For long in a new city. Popes and princesses asked me to dine.
When Catherine the Great demanded my company, I declined
On account of her lax morality. I thought her a glorified courtesan.
Joseph of Austria was a true compatriot: not a month on the
    throne
And he'd visited every prison and hospital, sometimes with only a
    footman.

I was summoned by the Roman Fisherman. He was
    non-committal.
I know you Englishmen do not value these things,
But the blessing of an old man can do you no harm. I kissed his rings.
Then ignoring decorum, inspired by the Lord,
I mentioned my time with the Inquisitor General
Of Valladolid of Spain. He was gravely discomforted.

Shall my tongue be tied from speaking the truth
By any earthly king? To term that court, by an ingenious ruse,
The HOLY Inquisition, was a monstrous abuse.
I saw its instruments: Scavenger's Daughter, Little Ease.
I took tea in a room with a garrulous oil painting, smooth
As sin, of 97 heretics on fire in a procession. Even the breeze

Was painted as a victory. And this was what had to stop.
This table wrapped in black cloth with a Bible on it
Used to draw blood. This braying intolerance.
Power in the clotting of candle wax and confessions at midnight.
The Osnabrück Torture. The Terror of insignias. Pomp.
This being underground. We had to let in the light.

5

A lone voice in the wilderness? Perhaps.
But I wasn't a desert prophet. I didn't spin a vision out of nothing,
Not attempt the Celestial City without researching everything.
I looked where long centuries had averted their gaze.
I made the commonest filth—the swarming of dungeon rats—
A suppurate state malaise.

My plan was simple, practical, and above all, cheap.
Salary the turnkeys. No profits to be gleaned from pimping,
Turning barman, extortion, or doctoring
In ignorance and at extravagant expense. No fees
For removing leg irons, access to the fireplace, or supplying cheese
    and meat.
No garnish to be sought off new arrivals. No hierarchies.

If idleness breeds vice, industry brings a smiling account balance
And the promise of self-sufficiency. Attach a factory,
A cloth works or a smelting house, to every penitentiary.

Let every inmate be supervised there. Out of such labour,
An income for provisions, heating, clothing and medicine, in
accordance
With daily needs. Allow extra for good behaviour.

I came home famous. *The State of the Prisons* such a manifest success
It engendered an Act of Parliament. Yet all along,
Sickness was festering in my only son like sedition in a nation
With a missing king. The French Revolution unfurled across the
Channel
As the desperate hints of scandalised servants converged into flesh
And betrayal. They boy was irrecoverable.

What example had I inculcated by wallowing in evil?
My absence gave licence to the deviant Thomasson,
Who defiled himself with numberless men, at dockside brothels in
London,
Taking his charge along with him.
The boy contracted venereal disease, ravaged by the Devil
In a butler's turncoat. Syphilis had already attacked my son's facial
skin

By the time I finally encountered him, flailing and spitting in my
hallway.
Demented with hatred. Pretence was useless, sophistry over,
As he raved he had known neither father nor mother,
That I had twisted him with neglect. I wept. He was destined for an
asylum.

Must reform cost exponentially? My conscience sears me, as with

    David I say:

O my son Absalom, my son, my son.

6

To ten poor families, who for ten long years
Have refused to visit an alehouse, five pounds.
Let us look to the regeneration of souls.
Assign every prison a chapel, and a chaplain.
Those who swing from the scaffold to inculcate fear
Are not only lost to Christ, they are lost to the Nation—

To its mines, and battlefields. *To ten more families,*
Not receiving parish funds, most constant
At church attendance, five pounds. Watch
All inmates ceaselessly. Ensure that the sexes are segregated,
And that prisoners are confined in sexual purity
By sleeping on their own. Let even their dreams be inspected.

To twenty poor widows, two guineas.
Let time be spent thinking of trespass.
Of what went wrong. And why. Teach them to ask forgiveness
So they can emerge from solitude like butterflies from a chrysalis.
Lead them to the wall of self-discovery
Which they will bleed upon, before they see their faces

Shining back at them. *One hundred pounds for the poorest prisoners*
Throughout the county gaols. No more haemorrhaging

The poor to Australia. No more rotting
On hulks along the Thames, as though this were the answer.
The people can be reclaimed, with ardour,
To their rightful inheritance. Making order stronger.

Five hundred pounds to a new society
For alleviating the miseries of public prisons
After my time is done. I have burned a single instance
Of concern, I do not trust Parliament as keepers of the flame
When I have vanished into heaven. Found a reform league to defy
Their wisdom. Mark it with my name.

My son to have whatever remains.
So much that I have left undone. And so much harm.
I shut out his invective, and instead return
To the obedient child, who stayed on until four, when darkness fell.
His frozen, painful hands were raw for days.
I kiss them well.

FROM

THROUGH THE SQUARE WINDOW

(2009)

STORM

It was already Gothic
enough, what with that
King of Versailles–sized bed
with room for me and two
or three liveried footmen;

wall-lights like candle-shafts
in fake pearl and cut
glass; and the stranded
little girl in the photographs
growing sorrowful—

her cascade sleeves, her floral
crown—as though taken
by Lewis Carroll. All afternoon
the church bells rang out
their warning. Cumulostratus

ascended into heaven.
Evening and the white forked
parting of the sky fell
directly overhead, casements
rattled on hinges and Thunder

may as well have summoned
the raggle-taggle denizens
of his vociferous world:
the ghouls, the gashed, the dead
so bored by now of being

dead they flock to gawk—
sanctuary was still sanctuary
except more so, with the inside
holding flickeringly, and the
outside clamouring in.

MATTER

FOR S.P.

Aristotle observed and recorded it all—
that out of rainwater, the marrow
of the human spine, foam from the sea,
or the putrefying carcasses of bulls and horses
spring living beings: frogs, serpents, anchovies,
bees and scarabs, locusts, weevils, maggots.
St Augustine agreed: what matter that the smallest
(and most meddlesome) of God's creatures
find no mention in the chronicle of the Ark?
So long as alluvial mud remained, or rotted
wood, or rinsed white bones of crocodiles
after the wash abated and the salvaged couple
and their braying entourage were pitched
on top of Ararat, wasps and gnats and fleas
would manifest once more in clouds and colonies
without a union of the sexes (like Mary)
and the earth would effortlessly teem.
Recipes for rats and 'small white puppies
a child might play with' followed
during the Middle Ages, which typically included
hay, excrement, dirty shirts, wool

simmered for an hour then hung to dry

in an outhouse or chicken coop

(the air of such places being itself

so mutable and laden with infusoria,

it acts as a bridge to life). Golems

moulded from clay still needed a spell

to keep them animated, as though by

growing bigger and more complicated,

the offspring of the elements

were in danger of winding down,

yet Paracelsus, arch-advocate of decay,

saw no reason not to apply

the laws of spontaneous generation

to ourselves: *let the semen of a man*

putrefy by itself for forty days in a sealed

cucurbite, it shall begin, at last, to live.

Fed on an arcanum of human blood

and kept in darkness, his fleet homunculus

had all the features of a human child.

Leeuwenhoek bore this experiment in mind

when, decades later, using his own microscope,

he scrutinised his sperm, magnified

as much as three hundred times and fashioned

like a bell, with the wrought perfection

of a tiny man curled inside each globule.

Ovists may have envisaged instead

a sacred cabinet of children, encased

inside each egg, opening in time
both backwards and forwards
to the breaking of Eve and the End
of the World, the likelihood remained:
whether one believed in this, or the evidence
of a light-balanced workshop and a knack
for polished glass, or whether one went back
to what the Greeks expressed
as the facts of reproduction,
a woman's quest for contraception,
stacked against the odds of dogged visitors
finding lodging in the womb
at any beckoning, was hopeless.
No wonder Soranus suggested water from Blacksmiths'.
No wonder olive oil, the pulp of a pomegranate,
honey, pine resin, mercury, beeswax,
pennyroyal, tobacco juice, arrowroot, tansy
were burnt, brewed, inhaled, ingested,
inserted into the cervix, or buried in fields left fallow
if the coppery stain of menstruation
persisted into the seventh day.
No wonder witches consulted the sky.
And though I know, thanks in part to Pasteur—
to his gauze impediments and penchant
for boiling—how you came to enter,
how you came to roll and hiccup and kick
against the windowless dark, feet to my heart

and skull to the pelvic cradle, I still think
of our lovemaking as a kind of door
to wherever you were, waiting in matter,
spooled into a form I have not yet been shown
by the unprompted action of nature,
by something corrupting in an earthenware pot
in Corinth, say, or Kingstown.
Stay the wind on a river eight weeks after equinox—
witness blue-green mayflies lift off
like a shaken blanket; add algae
and alchemical stones to the lake floor
in the strengthening teeth of winter, what swans.

RETURNING FROM ARIZONA

Back from the kiln-fired punishment of Mars
      where humans cannot live
      except indoors or in air-conditioned cars
and roadside shrines show Jesus in his crib

with a black face even in summer,
      our plane descends
      through a vapourish downpour:
the now-usual August deluge of these islands.

Rain smears the windows. Rivers have overshot
      their mark and fields
      for miles around the airport
sport pewter lakes. A heron stands by a cattle shed.

Getting too much of what you've acutely missed
      too suddenly
      —the median notion botched—
can render you wary of wishing's blunt chicanery:

like longing for weeks to be sick
      to prove the baby's taken,
      then failing to find a tonic
for another being's foothold in your person.

FOUND ARCHITECTURE

FOR KERRY HARDIE

These days are all about waiting. What would you say
if I tried to explain how my single true activity
this wet and shivery May is 'found architecture'?

As the giver of an Italian kaleidoscope
that makes its heel-toe shapes, not from beads or seeds
or painted meticulous details, but from the room,

from whatever room I happen to be in,
or from the street, always eager and unerringly
democratic, you stand slightly to the south of me

with your head raised and I imagine you smiling.
The day it arrived I mangled the blue of the bathroom
with the pistachio green of my bedroom ceiling

and sat entranced: such symmetrical splicing
of everything, anything, to make of my waiting-house
a star-pointed frame that entered and left

itself behind as the cylinder turned. Any light that there was
was instantly mystical—a crack in the pattern's
typography, like the door at the end of the corridor

shedding radiance. Yesterday evening, by the sea,
a strangled sealed-off swamp by a walkway
threw up, suddenly, the Aboriginal outback:

rotted glands of a pond between knee-high grasses
and a white tree undoing itself in its ink-stained
surfaces. The tree looked like a crocodile's rib cage

as I passed along the perimeter, or the wide-propped
jawbone of a whale. Until it became, the further
I walked, a canoe, asleep on the water and fettered

with algae. Another dead branch sat up
in the grass like the head of an otter and talked.
This, too, was found architecture. And all the usual,

of course: skeletons of geranium leaves on windowsills
long afterwards; snakeskins, clouds.
Beaches are full of it: found architecture being

the very business of beaches. Most recently
(and most disarmingly) this: handed to me in a roll
of four like mug-shot photographs from a machine—

his seahorse spine, his open-shut anemone
of a heart, and the row of unbelievable teeth
shining high in the crook of his skull as though backstitched

into place. From blood and the body's
inconsolable hunger I have been my own kaleidoscope—
five winter-bleached girls on a diving board, ready to jump.

VANITY FAIR

Dearest William—

I could begin by hoping you are well in England
(and I do!) now that the ——th regiment has returned
to Chatham; or I could begin by telling you
that reports of worsening weather here are true;
that Georgie thinks you wicked and unkind
for leaving him; that your former servants pine;
or that Father, though no better, is no worse, etc.
But this is not a weather-talk sort of letter.
It is after three. The whole house sleeps
(even Becky) and I am kept awake six weeks
by your crippling absence: an irony, I confess,
since for all your years of passionate presence
I failed to cherish you . . . Now that you're gone,
Becky (and you were right about her all along)
keeps dreadful company: boorish men who jest
and drink and flirt and she isn't in the slightest
shocked by any of it. I keep to my room.
I have placed the portrait of George facedown
on the dresser. I have folded the gloves you left
in an innermost drawer, as though they were a gift.
Since you spoke of my *incapacity* for love
I have come to see how my own fierce widowhood

was a shell against the world, a kind of carapace
made up of pride, stupidity and cowardice,
a stay, if you will, against 'the kind of attachment'
such as yours for me deserved. Poor shredded raiment—
for if it did not keep me warm, it kept me safe,
safe against you and safe against myself.
Last year, at the opera (it was *Dido and Aeneas*),
I wished to take your hand—in a sudden, artless,
harmless way that would not give you pause—
then didn't. I think I must have sensed the charge
built up from a decade's loving in your fingers
(though there you sat, as solid as an anchor)
and feared that touching it would knock me flat.
Now I'm scared I shall die without it.
Dear Dobbin, come back. Like everything else we do
in our mingled, muddy lives, this letter is overdue.
Forgive me if my love arrives belatedly,
but there is a ship can get you here by Friday
and, come all the rain in Christendom,
I shall be waiting for you by the viewing platform.
Dearest William, put out to sea.

Yours, Amelia Sedley

APOCRYPHA

When I was ten and convinced
I would never have children

simply by keeping my underwear on
at night-time, I was disarmed

by the history
of Mary Ann Sexton—

mother, camp-follower, picker
of pockets, stower of teeth—

and of how her womb
was pierced by a bullet

still wet from the testicle
of a Roundhead lieutenant

at the Battle of Marston Moor.
As though the slaughter itself

required climax and sought out
the unlikeliest agents, or

a new king pined
to be born, this was as improbable

a conception
as the physical laws of the earth

and all the revolving planets
could allow.

What hope was underwear now?
If destiny hovered

with green wings and a stained,
indefatigable purpose

over my bedspread,
I, too, would be done for.

ICE

They've come & gone before.
        Two hours or so
of a fine rain freezing on impact
        & what passes
for the world in West Quebec
        (woods, sugar-
bush, pylons, sheep) has spangled
        itself in ice.
Branches bend & snap & forests
        for years afterwards
hold their grieving centres bare
        where Pin Oak,
Siberian Elm, Common Hackberry
        & Bradford Pear
perform a shorn prostration & are
        unable to right
themselves; they teach the weeping
        willow how it's
done. Sometimes Frost's broken
        dome of heaven
is how storms end, just that, a shattering
        in the sunlight
of the million crystal filaments
        that fell & hung

on everything, as though absence of
breath had caused
the general lock-in & simple breath
was all we ever
needed to un-sleeve the present
& make it real again.

★

Monday, January 5th: we wake
to a bluish light
lasering through the window, a wiped
display on the radio
& the racket of gunshot. The house
is cold & all
around the trees are coming down.
First the crack
at the stem of the weight-sore trunk,
then a clinking
magnified, a china shop up-ending
in an earthquake,
as the branches rattle & snag.
When the whole
tree hits, a volley of shots goes up
& its burden of glass
explodes. This ten, twenty, fifty times
until we lose each crash

to the cacophony of the week-long storm.
   I still remember
you standing in your housecoat
   that first night
& how your face was lit by the
   transformer
shorting out outside. We didn't know
   the blackout
ended five states wide, or that the
   footprint
of the ice-storm could be seen
   from space.

*

The sheep were dead. The summary
   execution
of every maple within earshot
   finally stopped
at dawn on the penultimate day.
   The house still
stood, astonished, the one upright
   among a litter
of horizontals, & while it rained
   & froze, rained
& froze, a quiet inside the rainfall
   began to

spread itself abroad, all targets down,
    all debris blown
asunder. You begged me to check
    the sheep.
I knew before I reached them two
    hours later—
the outline of my person hanging
    frozen in the air—
that none of them had survived.
    The silence
was ubiquitous & pure as star-silence.
    So all I had
to offer as I slipped & slithered home-
    wards was an out-
building of kneeling, petrified sheep,
    locked to their
spots like pieces in a Snow Queen's
    game of chess.

                    *

Frost flowers. Bearded trees. Ghosts
    of some sudden
deleterious fungus ballooning out
    of the brushwood
one spectacular rose-bowl morning
    the previous

fall. The lavish, sexual freeze
        of long-stemmed
plants whose ensuing ersatz petals
        splinter when
touched. Midnight, January 9th:
        the jettisoned
excess of the Mississippi Delta
        had punished
us enough. Rain reverted to gas. Before
        the burials, before
the muddy thaw, before the gathering
        mass of melted ice
flooded the south, before the army
        & the extraction
of what was felled from what was
        left, we stood
at our living-room window & watched
        a tiny moon
& a tatter of stars high up in the
        atmosphere
& kissed as two will kiss through sheets
        dipped in dis-
infectant, & everything between us
        flew apart.

Love, the nightwatch, gloved and gowned, attended.
Your father held my hand. His hands grew bruised
and for days afterwards wore a green and purple coverlet

when he held you to the light, held your delicate, dented
head, thumbed-in like a water font. They used
stopwatches, clip charts, the distant hoofbeats of a heart

(divined, it seemed, by radio, so your call fell intertwined
with taxicabs, police reports, the weather blowing showery
from the north) and a beautiful fine white cane,

carved into a fishhook. I was a haystack the children climbed
and ruined, collapsing almost imperceptibly
at first, then caving in spectacularly as you stuttered and came

—crook-shouldered, blue, believable, beyond me—
in a thunder of blood, in a flood-plain of intimate stains.

The only places he can dive to are the senses.
The Christmas lights his father dangled from the corners
of his ceiling in July are his palimpsest for the world—
a winking on and off of ebullient colour, unnamed and so untamed,
to be committed to memory and then written over.
For now the world is simply to be crawled into, like the sea,
of which he has no fear, a bubbling, transmogrifying, all-
attracting mechanism that has not yet disappointed
with the mean-spirited vanishing act of an ink-black horizon.
He has already learned how the tongue contains more mystery
than the granite hulk of an elephant swaying suddenly into focus
under the dank and knotted overhang of Cave Hill, tossing
straw onto its shoulders to keep itself warm because it still
—and tragically—remembers Africa, that when he opens
his mouth to admit the spoon, anything can happen,
from passion fruit to parmesan. The three tributary-
sounds of his name that flow as one (as though summer's
hottest month had a feminine ending) he knows, and the purring
of cats and cars and the howling of dogs and fireworks.
His fingers adjust the tufts of the sheepswool coat
he lies on in his sleep. Tomorrow I'll offer him the dent
of a worry stone and the fluted sticky centres of acacia flowers.
All this can only be where he goes—there can be no other possibility—
unless we accept that memory begins in the womb or back,

still further, in the undiscovered bourne poor Hamlet dreamed

~~of entering without map or compass as a deliverance~~

from the sight of our back garden in September, the apple tree

keeled over and cankered and the fuchsia disrobed.

If he ever bombs inside a swimming-pool, or deep-sea dives,

or moon-walks, if he ever moves from balancing

on some underwater floor, precariously filled with air,

to pressing off on the balls of his feet into his own ascent,

through a dense and illegible element, he may remember

what it felt like to wake when he was one, and that it was

a slow, alert surfacing towards the morning, the clock's face,

the seagulls and the sea's address, all clamouring to be experienced.

THROUGH THE SQUARE WINDOW

In my dream the dead have arrived
to wash the windows of my house.
There are no blinds to shut them out with.

The clouds above the Lough are stacked
like the clouds are stacked above Delft.
They have the glutted look of clouds over water.

The heads of the dead are huge. I wonder
if it's my son they're after, his
effortless breath, his ribbon of years—

but he sleeps on unregarded in his cot,
inured, it would seem, quite naturally
to the sluicing and battering and paring back of glass

that delivers this shining exterior . . .
One blue boy holds a rag in his teeth
between panes like a conjuror.

And then, as suddenly as they came, they go.
And there is a horizon
from which only the clouds stare in,

the massed canopies of Hazelbank,
the severed tip of the Strangford Peninsula,
and a density in the room I find it difficult to breathe in

until I wake, flat on my back with a cork
in my mouth, bottle-stoppered, in fact,
like a herbalist's cure for dropsy.

The Plasterers: *The Creation*
The Cardmakers: *The Creation of Adam and Eve*

> The Fullers: *Adam and Eve in Eden*
> The Armourers: *The Expulsion*

The Shipwrights: *The Building of the Ark*
The Fishers and Mariners: *The Flood*

> The Parchmentmakers and Bookbinders: *Abraham and Isaac*
> The Pewterers and Founders: *Joseph's Trouble about Mary*

The Tilethatchers: *The Nativity*
St Leonard's Hospital: *The Purification*

> The Vintners: *The Marriage at Cana*
> The Cappers: *The Woman Taken in Adultery*

The Bakers: *The Last Supper*
The Cordwainers: *The Agony in the Garden and the Betrayal*

> The Bowers and Fletchers: *Christ Before Annas and Caiaphas*
> The Tapiters and Couchers: *The Dream of Pilate's Wife*

The Butchers: *The Death of Christ*

~~The Cooks and Waterleaders: *The Remorse of Judas*~~

    The Tailors: *The Ascension*

    The Potters: *Pentecost*

And episodes in between with a yet more fabulous cohabiting:

The Woolpackers and Woollenweavers: *The Assumption of the Virgin*

    The Spurriers and Lorimers: *Christ and the Doctors*

    The Spicers: *The Annunciation*, and

Because even a singing gash in the stratosphere is redeemable,

    The Fall of Man

To the repairers of barrels, buckets, and tubs.

Dear Heart, I dreamed a territory so seeming rich
and decorous, I woke with all its workings on my tongue.
Napoleon vanquished Europe. But when he died
(of natural causes) on the Palace-Garden Isle, Isola Bella,
built to resemble the rigging of ships, the map changed colour
from the Bay of Biscay to the Carpathian Peaks as bloodlessly
as the delicate octopus its rippling skin. The world shrugged off
his atheistic scarlet and dipped itself in yellow, the yellow of egg-
yolk and daylight's origin, and a Golden Age let down its iron
    bridge
and set us travelling. Everywhere was the same: commerce
was encouraged (though not excessively); order and cleanliness
governed and dignified both public and private realms; music
and poetry could be heard in all quarters. In Spain itself, the centre
of the Empire, all were as one: Language, Religion, the Crafts of
    State,
and the people flourished and were happy, the sap in the veins
of a Body Politick in rigorous health. Women, ever the lynchpin
of households and families, of the men who bear the imperial
    message
like a lamp into the dark, wore their mantle lightly, were softly
spoken, modestly attired, and thought at liberty to work and roam
abroad, turned all their passion inwards to their sons and homes . . .

travelling through Switzerland in a previous summer, we stopped
in Bern and witnessed the Zytglogge: a medieval tower of time.
Beneath its east main face is an intricate astronomical and
    astrological
device, wherein, in one small radius, are displayed:
all twenty-four hours, the hours of brightness, the days
of the week, our position in the zodiac, the date, the month, the
    progress
of the moon and the degree of elevation of the sun on the horizon.
It was raining that straightforward European rain we seldom see
at home and a small crowd murmured to their umbrellas
as Kaspar Brunner's parade of bears, Chronos with his hourglass,
and a grinning jester in cap and bells rattled out of the darkness
four minutes to the hour. And my dream was like this—
as these eight signposts to our mortal existences
clicked and chimed together, so the interlocking arms
of God and Man and Government danced flawlessly there.
What measure of exactness could keep my golden territory
intact and accurate to the second? That same year, but later,
a woman read my fortune in a brace of cards. One showed a cup,
for love, and another a blinded girl, and another a hill of wheels
and gibbets, stood stark against the sky as the Saviour's Cross.

FLU

When flu arrived that winter, I was ill for weeks.
Even my eyes were infected. I lay back and hallucinated—
the light was a flesh balloon; his face, when he came
with bitter effervescence, a bitten-through moon

or thigh bone . . .   After that, I slept
or stared at *A Century of Russian Photographs*.
Anastasia's chocolate frown. Lenin on his stack.
Lily Brik with her horseshoe teeth and headscarf.

And then page after page of unreadable scenes
I couldn't get the measure of, like the clusters of dots
in a magazine, containing a fortress
or Tyrannosaurus rex if you only knew how to lose focus.

The afternoons were quietest.
The streets outside my window held snow and letterboxes.

The fair had come. It must have been Whitsun.
They'd camp every year at the end of our yard—
you could hear the screams and the grinding of the rides
and a noise like whizz-bangs from the house.
Tom had taken Hazel off to get lost in it
so I had the kitchen to myself. Which was larger,
somehow, and scented, and lonely. I was baking scones.

It was Esther gave me the shock—*hello Doris*—
standing in the door-frame like a ghost.
She's been riding all afternoon: the dipper,
the dodgems, the giant wheel. You could tell
she was five months gone just by looking at her.
She needed the privy—*it would save me the walk*—
and I said all right because she was family.

She was out there an age. I had the scones in the oven
and the table scrubbed and the dishes washed
and draining on the rack and was wondering
if she'd stumbled on the garden path
when she came back, grey as a newspaper.
She put a hand to her hair and straightened her frock.
See you at church, then. Give Tom my best—

And then she left. I waited till the scones were finished,
dried my hands on a tea-towel, slipped my rings
from the windowsill, and made my way
past the rain barrel and the rabbit hutch to the door
of the outhouse, which was shut. Spiders' webs,
threaded like a lattice, covered the blistering paint.
I lifted the latch.

Inside, blood was everywhere: on the floor, on the walls.
You could tell where Esther had walked
by a set of white shadows. And then I saw her child—
bigger than the span of my hand and furred,
its fingers were curled near its ears and its eyelids were veined.
Its back was to the bowl. It was a girl.
I couldn't take my eyes off it, until I remembered

where I was and what had happened,
and stepped out onto the path and went back to the kitchen.
The sounds from the fair seemed louder
after that: hurdy-gurdy music and the cries of the ticket sellers
ratcheting up for the evening . . .
I sat at the table, waiting for Tom to come in.
The ceiling caught the colours of the machines.

Her father was born in Arkansas, the youngest, loneliest child
in a family of five. They lived in a four-roomed house
in a middle-sized town. When America went to war, he witnessed
columns of volunteers, filing out beyond the window,
singing, how fires on the street corners opposite blunted the night.
When his brothers got shot, he knew it was all his fault.

His mother was meticulous in punishment. So many faults
accrued to him, like interest, turning a fair-haired, freckled child
into a cross, she grew ingenious. If he wet the bed at night
(which he often did) she'd parade him through the house,
wrapped in a steaming sheet, to the frame of a backlit window,
so that people passing below might notice and be witness

to such wickedness. Other punishments went unwitnessed:
the confiscated meals, the bleeding feet. He was faulted
for speaking, and for keeping quiet. Mooning by the window
when his mother wasn't looking, he imagined himself a different
    child
in a different kind of country, Mexico perhaps, or Texas, in a house
that, barring moonlight, would be kept completely dark at night—

no standing lamps to shame him by . . . One night
while his parents slept, he ran away. There were no witnesses.
He left no note. He extracted himself from the house
like oil devolving itself from water, and found a job repairing faults
for the national telegraph company. Though still technically a child
(at seventeen) he knew this was his window

to the life he'd always dreamed of, a window
that would shut and lock before his twenty-first year. On a
    star-shot night
in Boulder, Colorado, he was married to Anne, who cried like a child,
while her father glowered beside them, their only witness.
The sex was her fault for being curious, the foetus her fault
that made her sick and saw them stuck in a four-roomed house

in a middle-sized town, so like the house
back home in Arkansas, his spirit failed him. Two small windows
stared onto the street. Anne grew silent, obedient to a fault.
Six months after the wedding, at ten past midnight,
Anne clutching the iron bedpost, the doctor arrived to witness
the birth of Mary Ruby Evans, their first and final child.

Whose fault that for twelve years afterwards in that house
a man slipped into the room of a child, kept back from the tiny
    window,
and nightly undid what only the hawk moths witnessed?

Once, a boy
with a bare brown chest
brought a hare to our back door.
It was heavy summer: the alleyway
he walked along held August's
bin-lid stink & stupor.
He wouldn't stay,

declared the hare
a present from his father.
My brother fetched a length of string,
tied it by its feet, then watched as our mother
fastened it carefully to the iron banister
where it spun like the spiralling
seed of a sycamore,

losing momentum . . .
Soon enough it hung there
motionless, impaled upon its own
frozen direct line of perfect martyrdom,
its eye an abyss, its foxglove fur
unblemished bar the torn
& matted abdomen

where the shot
went in. I could have sat
at the foot of the flight of stairs
for hours to get the measure of it (its ear-tips
dipped in black against the almost-white
of its ears' interiors!) if my mother
had allowed it.

She banished me
outside, where the afternoon
lay festering, & yet it almost seemed as if
the sunken playground, hacked-out stumps of trees
& blackened mattresses where a fire had been
were wiped out by this gift,
this legacy

of unimpeded air,
of whitethorn-quartered fields
for miles around, of granular traces
still on the skin from a swimmable river,
of plovers' eggs, the calyx-wheels
of larkspur, of spaces
where a hare

might flourish . . .

Like a sideshow hawker
with a star exhibit, I rounded in
the street, before my father skinned & washed
& jugged the hare in blood & butter.
Look, I said to a ring of children
& pointed. *It's gorgeous.*

CATHEDRAL

As though the world were a spiral staircase,
and the order in which you ascended it
already set, I wanted the words
you attempted first to be solid and obvious:
apple, *finger*, *spoon*. The bat
hanging like a blister in your drool-proof
baby book or the lovesick cricket
with its gossamer instrument
were surely to be held back:
until I could explain, until I could build
you a zoo of improbable candidates
and properly introduce you.
But you were too quick—
like panic, there was no stopping it—
each day's vast, unbreachable
impact—and language,
in whatever ramshackle order
it made its presence felt—
a movable moon, the guts
of a clock, a fire escape—
rained down and into you, like
Catherine Linton's wine-through-water
dream of the heath and expulsion
from heaven. I cannot hang

a curtain to keep it off. I cannot
section it. It is entering via
the ear's aqueduct, every
listening second, trickling in
to its base equilibrium
and carrying with it an image in negative
to be absorbed by the brain and stored.
Bah! humbug! you say, aged two,
like the terrible man
in the cape with the walking stick
you glimpsed in the afternoon,
and what we assumed you knew
is jolted on its axis; then this:
at six o'clock the ghost
of a child might come and eat porridge.
We are speechless.

DASH

Longer please!—two out of fifty usable words
you employ to hold us hostage—

longer in the cooling bath, longer
by the playground gates, mowing imaginary grass,

longer driving your car-cum-aeroplane—
and we want longer too—

and smaller boxes to fold your clothes into
or not to have to shed them at all—

but before we know what's hit us,
we're standing on the roadside, staring west

at the last of a trail of dust, like the crowds
who wait all day for a royal visit

for it to simply pass them by—
before they've memorised the hair, the eyes,

the inscrutable footmen, the marvellous horses

They're here to make money, the men distinguished
from the crowds they move among
by white hats and walking sitcks,
to capture as many people as possible
for their fairground bioscope shows.
Come see yourselves on the screen as living history!

And history sets up its Nordenograph and rolls
and vacuums in the girls in shawls, the men and boys in caps,
the entire rollicking sea
of spinners and doffers and little tenters
departing the factory gates at six
like a nation's exodus.

Everyone wears clogs. Everyone has a dinner to get to.
But the dock of a quarter-day's pay for a minute of horseplay
is no longer over their heads
and so they jostle, momentarily, blurred face by blurred face,
to smile or to bow, for the transmission of grace
in the space near the cinematographer

as though the camera cast out a fraught pool of light
in exchange for their imprint
and they are standing in it.
The women loiter less. A handful of men doff caps, then laugh
or shake incredibly white, wide handkerchiefs
at whoever may prove their witness:

themselves, their wives, coal miners, tram conductors,
Boer War veterans, Lloyd George in the wings—who knows—
the King—not to mention the unthinkable yet-to-be-born,
not to mention me. And always,
in every factory-gate frame,
like an offering up of driftwood

out of the indeterminate mass
after its comb and polish
or the crystallisation of salt from a smoky suspension,
children linger longest in the foreground,
shoving, lampooning, breaking the line,
or simply staring back at us, across the lens's promise,

as though we still held Passchendaele in our pockets
and could find a way to save them.
They grin and grin—*not yet, not yet*—
while in a corner of the screen, a cart horse stumbles,
flickers, flashes into darkness
where the cellulose nitrate stock rubbed off inside the milk churn.

SHADOWS IN SIBERIA
ACCORDING TO KAPUŚCIŃSKI

Are upright—
cast not by sunlight but by frozen breath:

we breathe
and are enveloped in an outline

and when we pass,
this outline stays suspended, not tethered

to our ankles
as our sun-shadows are. A boy was here—

fantastically dressed
against the arctic frost like an heirloom glass

in bubble wrap—
he has disappeared into the portico

of himself. Not even Alice,
with her knack for finding weaknesses

in the shellac
of this world, left so deft a calling card.

DON JUAN, 2012

DON JUAN, 2012

And money, that most pure imagination . . .

—Don Juan, Canto XII, 2, 7

I

We need a hero. The time is out of joint,
  has burnt its fragile socket, while for the Mayans,
who read their dazzling mountain stars like newsprint,
  transcribing mankind's pre-allotted lifespan—
by 2012, there's simply no more of it.
  God's eighteenth-century clock has winded down.
We're at the end, or so the websites warn us,
of everything we know and value precious.

I'm usually unconvinced, convinced instead
  that end-of-history talk is soon demolished
by history's own refusal to be led
  into some silent terminus. Things may not flourish:
we may be colder, hungrier, more upset
  by the growing list of what's been taken from us.
But even lame, thin, choking and at variance
with the riches of before, we'll falter on regardless.

Now I'm not so sure. Take this week's news:
     a cataclysm, a Herculean storm
unlike anything even Al Gore lent shape to
     is closing in, fueled partly by a shifting jet-stream,
partly by the pole-ice melting through—
     a rough beast rising as the oceans warm.
We watch its blue-white swirl by satellite
on flashy CNN, like spies on our own planet.

We watch it hit. They've timed it to the second.
     A waterproofed and clearly mad reporter
getting tossed across a junction by the wind,
     then back again, up to his calves in water,
tries to speak to us but his voice is drowned.
     The anchorwoman smiles and leaves him there,
shuttling between the leaning trees and the signals
as the rain rolls over him and the picture fails.

By morning, we're in Aftermath, a bird's-eye view:
     parks and streets submerged in the ravaged cities—
sheets of pewter sea blown into a new,
     transplanted element; kilometres of débris.
The north-east national grid has blown its fuse.
     The graces we now live by—transport, electricity—
that house us all in rooms of heated glass
lie savaged and defunct as the cable telegraph.

And how much will it cost? Dear Lord, the cost . . .

    Tens of billions, according to *The Guardian*,
on insurance claims alone for what's been lost.

    Since the financial crisis, we can't imagine
what so many profligate zeros, nestled close,

    reproduced like cells, have come to *mean*—
they march across our headlines, black and crass,
and always with a minus sign attached.

A little while ago in Houston, Texas,

    three awfully clever men invented something
very bold and deft and half-miraculous:

    a fresh, *creative* way to run accounting
(and why not?) whereby losses make a plus.

    They made wealth up: income, future earnings,
so that, sign without a signifier, wild
in its own unfettered realm, money multiplied . . .

. . . until it crashed. Oh what a falling off!

    While thousands lost their pensions, they went to jail
in handcuffs, though sadly not for long enough,

    and not before their brainchild had gone viral.
Soon debt became a bargainable stock

    and the trick with debt, how it loves to dive and spiral,
a ballooning asset. Champagne baths on Wall Street,

    the fizz of endless cash and nothing cheap,

not even escorts, a 'legitimate' expense,
  and certainly not the cars, the drugs, accessories
for adventure sports, the loft apartments.

  But holes are holes, no matter how unholily
they may be cloaked with crafty argument,
  and Enron's falling off just mere pinprickery
compared to the current void. A chasm splits
the contours of the earth. We're staring into it.

Like Attack of the Giant Crabs! The Killer Spiders!
  (small and normal creatures malformed by radiation)
all the hidden less-than-zero numbers,
  tired of being barred, like ruined cousins,
from civilised conversation, staged a takeover.
  We're starving, they announced, *and we are Legion.*
The mega-banks went first: their secret debts
devoured them from within, then spat them out.

The other banks we salvaged with our taxes.
  And for what? Their doors stay double-bolted
while talk of what we haven't got in practice
  is all the rage since money's lack revolted.
Nothing's offered: no credit, ready cash,
  no sweet forgiving margin; those evicted
from the homes they can't afford, who bought too late,
live someplace other than on ghost estates.

The outlook's bleak. We're inside a climacteric
    our baby boomer parents never dreamt of
who grew up in the groove of post-war pop music,
    who always had a job, who shared their love.
As weather forecasts grow apocalyptic,
    as doubting politicians lose their nerve,
as markets tumble, as what we're told we'll owe
engulfs our children's children—we need a hero.

11

A Judge? A Pope? A President? Not likely.
    Four years ago we thought we'd found a true one
when Obama won the White House. His wife was pretty,
    his daughters tall and modest; his speeches shone
like electroplated costume jewellery
    with glittering abstract nouns: *justice, freedom* . . .
But the poetry of campaigning got rearranged
as prose once he took office. Little changed.

Someone close to power but not wet-through
    with it; someone honest, wry, congenial,
who's commonplace enough to not be deaf to
    the voice of that most abstract noun, *the people.*
No banking magnate, no plane-and-shipping guru,
    no prophet of a lizard nation, no angel—
but best of all a mirror or a silver screen
we catch our captured selves reflected in.

Enter Donald Johnson. At sixty-three
     childless, virile, handsome, single, rich
with all the things he's done and where he's been
     (Australia, Budapest), still sleek and boyish,
still dynamic, still brim-full of bewitchery
     with women (who are still the ones to ravish
him) and who has recently found employment
as an attaché in the European Parliament.

To such a skilled adventurer, Belgium is dull
     (with compensations: waffles, chocolates, beer
so fine he quaffs it by the tankard-ful,
     mussels steamed in wine, shallots and butter,
stupendous *frites*) but on the whole he's grateful—
     a job's a job and he isn't getting younger.
He has a tiny flat above a park
and visits, *le weekend, Les Museés des Beaux-Arts.*

Work's a doddle. The mechanics of the Union
     grind and turn, down miles of spotless corridors
in countless shiny rooms. A gravy train
     for every sort of bureaucrat: directors,
policy advisors, inventors of Eurojargon
     (*Flexicurity, Acquis Communautaire*),
advocacy officers. The EU's sound:
it's well-oiled and its wheels go round and round.

He breakfasts with the Secretary at nine.
    He de-briefs after meetings those beneath him.
He drafts agendas, often before the deadline.
    He sets up conference calls in French and German.
He tracks reports and checks if stats align
    with various previous member-state projections.
He leaves at ten, to dine and then to bed
sometimes alone and sometimes with a friend.

And then things change. The map is not the territory
    and metaphor, like language, leaves a gap
between the thing described and its new summary.
    So when things change, metaphor plays catch-up.
A greased machine? The EU-as-a-Body's
    more apt now its economies are crap;
it ate a lot, in what they termed 'expansion',
then instantly fell foul of such infection

it threatens to expire . . . The U.S. sneezed,
    the EU caught the flu: national debts
so vast (and growing) they betray disease,
    rising unemployment, frozen assets,
tottering banks and shrinking GDPs.
    The five most gangrenous toes on Europe's foot—
Ireland, Italy, Portugal, Spain and Greece—
are losing blood and blackening from necrosis.

Surgeons stand ready, scrubbed and dressed in green.
　　Austerity! Austerity!—the answer
backed by Merkel, Europe's undisputed Sovereign—
　　has gripped us all ('we're all in this together')
but is gripping some like a slip-knot at a hanging.
　　Austerity the 'Fury' with 'abhorrèd shears'
who 'slits the thin-spun life'—the dreadful price—
the cutting off the nose to save the face . . .

It's Monday morning, dim with Brussels rain.
　　November 12th. The Secretary's serious.
He doesn't want to deal with the campaign
　　on Donald's list (a biodiversity crisis)
and stares into his coffee. News in from Spain
　　is dire, but the news from Greece disastrous
as Austerity cuts deep, cuts deeper still . . .
He wants a witness, someone with the skill

of staying low, anonymous and watchful,
　　to gather notes and keep him up to date
on how the current measures have proved harmful
　　(beyond the TV, papers and debates
in the two parliaments) to 'ordinary people'.
　　He spreads his hands. 'I'd like to delegate
this research trip to *you*, Mr Johnson.'
Call it a hero's quest, call it a mission—

Donald coughs and nods. Outside the window
    cherry trees in rows are almost bare:
the last of their scarlet/golden leaves to go
    before the winter, flash their burnished fire.
His ticket's booked. He'll leave for Greece tomorrow.
    The bleeding South. He's never been before
(but knows Lord Byron died there). He thinks of sun
and olives, wine with resin . . . Revolution.

III

Brussels' airport's busy with arrivals—
    a crisis brings the margins to the Centre
like supplicants to Rome. Its polished hall
    of cafés gleams and hums. Spice-in-sugar:
the caffeinated jazz of morning travel
    sets Donald tingling. He buys cologne, saunters
towards his departure gate, checks his watch,
then thinks of white geese ranged around a trough

with held-back wings as he stares at the jets outside.
    Hardly anyone's flying to Greece. No tourists.
No families steering buggies loaded high
    with snacks and nappies. No propertyists.
A bored EU official scans the sky;
    another suffers questions from a journalist
and by the entrance, a woman on her own
stands scrolling through a document by smartphone.

Donald looks again. Too long ago
     an interpreter for Russian sent a text
which conjured up the dear, well-worn scenario:
     dinner, drinks, a so-what-happens-next . . . ?
Perhaps a month. He mouths a warm hello
     across the seats, but she only seems perplexed
and looks away. She's dark, composed, elusive.
This only serves to make her more attractive.

The cabin's almost empty. Mozart trills
     to a frothy, crested peak—and down again.
Scattered heads observe the safety drill.
     Then the roar and lift of flight, the seat-belt sign
clicks off, and she's suddenly beside him in the aisle,
     asking if she can join him. Donald feigns
surprise and says of course. Not *over*-gleefully.
She stretches out her hand. 'I'm Persephone.'

She stows her laptop, feathers out her hair.
     He asks her if she makes this journey often.
She turns her gaze to his. 'Once a year.'
     They order wine—a lull before the conversation
loosens its tie and runs. 'Every winter,
     from November to February. I live in Athens.
And you, Mr . . . ?' 'Johnson. Call me Donald. Please.'
All is good. The flight's as smooth as a Baileys;

clouds are massed like floss beneath the wing-tip;
    sun is streaming in; she's friendly, smart,
with brilliant teeth and slightly glossy lips
    and could sweeten, not just the clockwork start
to this morning's flight but the whole brief trip . . .
    He muses on seduction, its lines, its parts,
its dartings forth, its keeping some things buried,
and mentally marks a tick for 'clearly interested'

as he listens to her talk. She talks a lot.
    And so the game of Working-Out commences.
She laughs and volunteers that she's a Eurocrat:
    a Master's in economics, fluent French,
a decade's stellar service (which makes her what,
thirty-five or six?—not, he thinks, on balance,
disturbingly his junior) and sent to oversee,
each winter, changes to the EU C.A.P.

in her own benighted country, on which she's expert.
    She wears no ring. 'It must be hard on your husband
when you leave?' She shrugs. 'He tolerates it:
    since we met, it's just what's always happened.
We lead our Belgian life, easy, quiet—
    not volatile, not raw-edged or impassioned—
and then I'm gone, and our winter lives are different
and we never ask precisely how they're spent.'

A husband—damn. But Oh the little thud
    in Donald's groin as she scurries to dispel him!
She's said enough, she's said more than she should
    if Donald doesn't rush to state his freedom
just as obviously. The flurry in his blood
    engulfs his knees. Is it the Sauvignon?
Is it the sun-drenched cloud-scape for a view?
He turns to her directly. 'I want you—'

and there's a moment then—she holds his stare,
    not moving, calm—and he listens to the engine
through the floor, and feels the pulse of her,
    as though they'd touched already, as though she'd spun
a web of silk and drawn him in. He falters,
    flutters closer (her mouth is slightly open)
and they kiss: a single quivering kiss,
and he's weirdly trapped like a climber in a crevice

as something rank runs through him, something cold
    from caverns too long shut to wind and light
deep inside the ground, where little grows
    but the thousand-year-long creep of stalactites
and fishless rivers carve out limestone folds
    and viaducts, and nameless shapes take flight—
He pulls away. The world is bright and stable:
here are his hands, here is his tray-table,

there's a suited woman smiling her assent,
    looking (slightly) embarrassed by his haste
but not affronted; they've started their descent.

    The seat-belt sign clicks on. 'That's a foretaste,'
she offers softly. Then she gathers her equipment
    and is gone—as though he'd dreamt her face,

her lips, the untold clammy depths of her . . .
Her perfume fills the air. Donald shudders.

IV

What is it we fear? We fear the loss
    of whatever it is we've set about our hearths
to keep life's slicing cold at bay: a house;

    a food supply; coins that hold their worth
from one day to the next; a health service.
    We fear the loss of a perpetually generous earth.

We fear the end of buses, the closure of stores,
we fear a return to conditions between the wars

when ragged men in lines brought all they owned—
    a battered bowl and spoon—to public kitchens;
when governments were fractured, jelly-boned,

    and hostage to a mass, enraged sedition
that ushered in such darkness, light was doomed.
    We fear a return to the Old Road into London

where mothers left their babies in the hundreds
to die of cold and lack of parish funds.

In 2012, on the 13th of November,
    all over Greece—in Athens, on the islands,
in the agricultural north—Loss is Ruler
    and only the slick and sheltered rich withstand
its hunger. Every flat, every schoolyard and taverna
    plays its host, and should the honeyed Sirens
still exist, their singing would be rent
with Greece's wailing, and turn into lament.

The airport's crazy. Just the day before
    a budget slashing billions, yet again,
from salaries and services was deplored
    around the Chamber, then passed by a squeaky margin.
Another national strike looms like a downpour.
    The rush to leave in advance of a total shut-down
is panic-stricken. Donald doesn't feel well.
He takes a taxi to a moderate hotel,

showers, cleans his teeth, and falls asleep
    in a room that's beige and redolent with smoke
and dreams a lake. He's standing ankle-deep
    and then he's flailing underwater and he chokes
and then he stops. He looks. Trapped—in reeds—
    a long-haired, staring girl . . . He jolts awake.
Outside on the street, two men are arguing.
Their voices play like scales: rising, falling,

rising . . . It doesn't end. The clock says eight.

He thought it would be earlier but the difference
in the hour? How did he sleep so late?

The room is dark. Headlights' luminescence
moves around the walls. He needs to eat,

shake off the wide-eyed girl, experience
the city in the evening, start making notes . . .
He stows his wallet and his phone inside his coat,

ignores the lift, trips down the dusty stairs,

and is in the lobby, striding towards the exit,
when he sees her—straight-backed in an armchair,

waiting. She's changed: no longer in a suit
but in a dress, not wearing make-up, older.

He'd told her nothing, now he thinks of it:
nothing about his life, his job, the reason
for the trip. Did she *follow* him?

'Mr Johnson—' She's stood to stop him leaving.

He brushes past. 'I'm here to introduce
you to the current facts. My car is waiting.'

And the strangeness of the day—its working loose
of steady, regular stuff (read *sleep* and *kissing*)

like a tongue around a half-extracted tooth—
goes up one notch. He finds himself disarmed,
inside her car as the door is being slammed,

Persephone beside him in the back,
    a wordless driver skulking in the front,
the night, both brightly lit and densely black,
    unravelling by his window, and what he wants
to say—*how dare you*—vanishing like a snowflake
    on a spit. He tries to speak but can't.
Athens seems normal: lovers hand-in-hand;
illuminated bars; tobacco stands—

like any typical European capital
    with tree-lined avenues of modern flats;
market squares packed tight with canvas stalls;
    displays of jewels and shoes and sequinned hats
gleaming in the darkness; a City Hall
    fronted by gushing fountains. Though there are rats:
he spots one as they angle round a corner,
flashed up by the headlights, then another—

then another—fast and fat and freakish—
    running out of pipes or into drains—
the streets are twitching. Tottering piles of rubbish
    begin to catch his eye. They turn again
into a major thoroughfare. He hadn't noticed,
    but garbage bags are everywhere: thrown
in heaps round litter bins, clogging doorways—
the refuse of a city, left for days . . .

'Welcome to the Winter of our Discontent.

   It's lasted years but now it's getting worse.

We borrow double, for every Euro spent.

   There's a bottomless pit in place of the public purse

that can't be filled, though each successive government

   tries its best. This is our constant curse,

like Sisyphus.' Sirens tear the air.

She leans forward in her seat. 'Syntagma Square.'

v

Syntagma Square, Syntagma Square's on fire

   Boots and batons, petrol bombs and bricks

They've strung up Merkel's portrait on a wire

   They've burned the German flag for bitter kicks

They've dumped the Euro symbol on the pyre

   and asked police to suck their fucking pricks

It's blazing, it's amazing, it's a whirl

with teargas and cannons, down in the underworld—

What do you get if you slice a loaf in half,

   then half, then half again? Answer: hungry.

What do you get if you lay off half your staff,

   the public civil servants of your country,

then threaten to axe the rest? Wheat from chaff,

   or the sudden, icy plunge into 'mere anarchy'?

You face two doors: an 'out'-door and an 'in'-door;

their signs are hidden, but both of them are trapdoors.

Eight little Indians, gayest under heaven—
  (seven little Indians, chopping up sticks)
one went to sleep, then there were seven—
  (one chopped himself in half and then there were six)
And there's never any chance of getting even
  And the wings to lift you out of here are wax—
One little Indian, left all alone,
he went out and hanged himself and then there were none—

The roar increases. A camera crew retreats.
  The riot squad advances like a wall.
Huddled against Persephone, Donald sweats.
  He doesn't want to stay with her at all
but there's smoke and screaming out there on the streets
  and he doesn't know the way to his hotel . . .
As though she's made her point (or read his mind),
she clears her throat, the car backs round a bend

then screeches off, untouched. They roll along
  past empty restaurants, strings of shuttered shops,
an ambulance growing fainter like a song
  on a turned-down radio, until it stops.
Persephone says: 'Disorder will go on—
  they'll broadcast it as students versus cops—
but it's everyone. The people have no choice.
They're damned already.' Donald finds his voice:

'Where are we headed to next?' 'A quiet place—'
    (Oh the relief of that!) 'To a garden.'
They're there in minutes: a residential space
    between two railway lines, overgrown
with weeds and shards and dubious sorts of waste—
    the kind of neglected by-pass, gypsy-rotten,
where immigrants begin their new existence
overlooked by us. Except there's silence:

no lights on in the flats; no smells of cooking;
    no children on the swing that someone's improvised;
no beat-up vans or bikes, no tethered washing.
    'Who were they?' 'These were Syrians, terrorised
by Assad, and his overindulged-in bombing
    of hospitals and schools. But Greece is immunised—
Europe's most porous border no longer leaks:
we round them up and house them all in concrete,

thirty to a cell—Iraqis, Afghans—
    and if they come by boat, our coast patrols
do their damnedest to ensure they never land.'
    A train grinds by, transparent as a fishbowl,
its passengers bright and separate, elsewhere-bound,
    who stare ahead. The wind is moaning cold.
A front door hanging slant like a flap of skin
bangs and bangs . . . Persephone sits waiting.

'There's one last site, a temple, we should visit—
    out at Sounion. Let's get started.'
And they drive. He finds her stern and forthright:
    the woman on the plane, a lie imparted
according to his known pre-requisites;
    a satin mask. *Among the dear departed,*
she shall reign: cruel, true, unwavering;
she carries out the curses of the living

upon the souls below and knows no anguish . . .
    This rings inside his head like burning scripture.
Soon Athens' dish of radiance is eclipsed.
    The road winds up through trees, they park, and there—
a roofless columned hall upon a cliff,
    the sea beneath—a drop of sixty metres—
sighing on the stones. 'Lord Byron came
and in the marble chiselled out his name,

but to us this place is famous for Aegeus,
    father of Theseus, who forgot to change his sails
from black to white. Although he returned victorious
    from the labyrinth, his father thought he'd failed:
he glimpsed the ship and, frenzied with distress,
    jumped from the cliff and gave this sea its name.'
Donald surveys the wide and smooth Aegean,
the temple's broken tribute to Poseidon,

wind plucking at his coat and at his hair,
  and wonders why they're there. 'Since last year,
suicide in Greece has grown more popular—
  wives and daughters, sisters, nephews, brothers—
instances have doubled. Some favour here:
  it's desolate and high, without a barrier,
and, like Aegeus, they strew the sea beneath them
with what is left when all their hope is done.'

VI

And yet the wretched truth is this: Byron
  might summon a hero (however much he meant it)
to play the leading role in his *Don Juan*,
  to be seduced and fight; we cannot.
To be lucky both in war and amongst women
  in nineteenth-century Europe *could* have cut it
(even if, in Juan's case, it didn't)—
for royalty was useless (the hapless Regent),

untrammelled aristocracy in its cups,
  and the old bone-house of influence, glued
with noble blood, finally coming unstuck . . .
  One could be dashing, magnetic, brave, imbued
with rhetorical gifts and almost incredible luck
  and make things happen—a king's false pledge come true;
a fairer treaty drafted; a people freed.
One could be dramatic. God knows change was needed

and God knows change is also needed now—

    but the new bone-house of influence's been rebuilt

with corporations' cash; it won't allow

    outsiders to invade; it's defended to the hilt

and ruled by those with savvy media know-how.

    Governments bow to Businesses; Businesses sit

secure behind closed doors and ruminate

on how to best direct affairs of state.

We might run our story's *dénouement* as follows:

    like scenes of Dickens' Ghost-of-Christmas-Present,

Persephone's display of Greece's sorrow

    works its full effect: Donald's incandescent.

He hurries back to Brussels, his soul aglow

    with a people's undeserved and cruel treatment

at the hands of the prosperous North . . . He barges in

on the Secretary's weekly Eurocrisis meeting,

demands an instant audience, *tête à tête*,

    and there unfurls a tale so sad, so shocking,

of a country where, if EU terms are met,

    everything goes to the dogs: law, policing,

the vestiges of a shredded welfare net

    to catch the unemployed and stop them starving—

the Secretary sighs. 'It's just as I suspected,'

he says when Donald's finished; 'It must be stopped'—

and while he's on the phone the camera switches
   to other phones which ring along the chain
in quick succession: a woman frowns, then flinches;
   a man listens, bangs his desk, then dials in turn
his own boss higher up . . . And so, like stitches
   cast on one by one, what Donald's seen
accumulates its own materiality,
grows real and vivid, felt; and in the sanctity

of the EU's topmost echelons, in blood-wet gowns,
   Austerity's merry surgeons down their scalpels.
Let's say we discover a brand-new Maynard Keynes:
   a no one up to now, a minor detail
in the ECB's machinery—good on loans
   and fiscal policy generally—who has an apple-
moment, an insight, a hot Eureka!-flash
and proposes simply *giving* Greeks more cash,

to spend just as they like, side-stepping banks.
   What would happen? The banjaxed wheels of commerce
could re-start; hand-outs be outflanked
   by the sale of goods; an ever-increasing workforce
pay their taxes . . . Who forms a one-man think-tank,
   which quickly grows and soon becomes the source
of *the* most radical EU plan in years:
a means for Greece to thrive without arrears

. . . But this is fancy. Donald wakes once more
    in his muted room at nine the following morning.
She must have dropped him back; he can't remember.
    His head is sore. The day is waiting—
a whole bright day to walk about without her—
    and he's glad: her doleful talk of keening,
of savagery set loose and baited traps
has made him sick and might not quite be accurate—

Greece might shine completely differently
    in daytime. And he's starving. The breakfast's good
(yoghurt, honey, fruit and fried *haloumi*)
    and puts him in an optimistic mood,
fuelled by several cups of shot-gun coffee.
    He feels the way he usually does abroad:
inquisitive, free, undaunted, at his ease,
alert to pretty women (who aren't Persephone),

ready to explore. There's no museum staff,
    which means the great Acropolis is shut,
as is the home of Agamemnon's mask,
    of Santorini's frescoes, Nestor's cup . . .
But there are ships and islands. To Aegina perhaps?
    The ferry smokes, the anchor gets wound up,
Piraeus shrinks then falls off the horizon,
Donald inhales the salt of the churning ocean,

seagulls scream and dive in the ferry's wake,

   the winter sunlight's pale but trails its touch

abundantly, everywhere he looks,

   in the white waves' ruffled scrim, the masthead's torch.

He feels inside his pocket for his notebook,

   flicks it open. He hasn't written much:

'Athens', the date. Then, to be rid of her,

he adds her name and casts it on the water.

PARALLAX

(2013)

PARALLAX: (*Astron.*) Apparent displacement, or difference in the apparent position, of an object, caused by actual change (or difference) of position of the point of observation; *spec.* the angular amount of such displacement or difference of position, being the angle contained between the two straight lines drawn to the object from the two different points of view, and constituting a measure of the distance of the object. —*Oxford English Dictionary*

1801

A beautiful cloudless morning. My toothache better.
William at work on The Pedlar. Miss Gell
left a basket of excellent lettuces; I shelled
our scarlet beans. Walked out after dinner for letters—
met a man who had once been a Captain begging for alms.

★

The afternoon airy & warm. No letters. Came home
via the lake, which was near-turquoise
& startled by summer geese.
The soles on this year's boots are getting worn.
Heard a tiny wounded yellow bird, sounding its alarm.

★

William as pale as a basin, exhausted with altering . . .
I boiled up pears with cloves.
Such visited evenings are sharp with love
I almost said *dear, look*. Either moonlight on Grasmere
                                        —like herrings!—
or the new moon holding the old moon in its arms.

In other noises, I hear my children crying—
in older children playing on the street
past bedtime, their voices buoyant
in the staggered light; or in the baby
next door, wakeful and petulant
through too-thin walls; or in the constant
freakish pitch of Westside Baltimore
on *The Wire*, its sirens and rapid gunfire,
its beleaguered cops haranguing kids
as young as six for propping up
the dealers on the corners, their swagger
and spitfire speech; or in the white space
between radio stations when no voice
comes at all and the crackling static
might be swallowing whole a child's
small call for help; even in silence itself,
its material loops and folds enveloping
a ghost cry, one I've made up, but heard,
that has me climbing the stairs, pausing
in the hall, listening, listening hard,
to—at most—rhythmical breathing
but more often than not to nothing, the air
of the landing thick with something missed,
dust motes, the overhang of blankets, a ship
on the Lough through the window, infant sleep.

SHADOWS

My shadow this morning on the station platform
looks impossibly stretched and beaten thin:
a stiltwalker's shadow, all legs and no torso;
a dun metal casing left after a hammering.

Late February sunlight, winter's filigree
still inside it. Beside me the bins
are casting vast apparitions
of themselves over the yellow line

while my head has lain itself down
across the tracks, the way it wanted to
all those years ago, in Amsterdam,
near the Leidesplein, before the see-through

boy with his quiver of arrows
could claim me as his own.
It jolts bolt upright as the Carrickfergus train
vanishes in the opposite direction.

I could be a dissident in a textbook in Soviet Russia
discovered after the print run
and painstakingly blackened out by each teacher,
or a stage set after the lights have blown

on a tinkly Victorian performance in reds and golds.
I could be blood in a black-and-white video.
The platform is shining with salt.
My shadow displaced at the waist is taking a bow.

Lady other, Lady mine, if I stood here all morning
I'd watch you retracting back like drowning soap.
Shadows of candles on church walls at Evensong
manifest not as flame, but smoke.

SHOSTAKOVICH

The wind and its instruments were my secret teachers.
In Podolskaya Street I played piano for my mother
—note for note without a music sheet—while the wind
in the draughty flat kept up: tapping its fattened hand
against the glass, moaning through the stove, banging
a door repeatedly out on the landing—
the ghost in the machine of Beethoven's *Two Preludes
Through All the Major Keys*, that said they lied.

Later I stood in a wheat field and heard the wind make music
from everything it touched. The top notes were the husks:
fractious but nervous, giddy, little-voiced,
while underneath a strong strange melody pulsed
as though the grain was rigging, or a forest.

In all my praise and plainsong I wrote down
the sound of a man's boots from behind the mountain.

PHOTOGRAPHS OF BELFAST
BY ALEXANDER ROBERT HOGG

The year the Great Ship Herself
is fitted out
at the mouth of the Lagan,

her panelling
drilled through and threaded
with miles of electric cables

and her gymnasium
horses finally bolted
down—

fifty cubic tonnes
of soot
falls over the city

in drifts, in rain, in air
breathed out then in again,
re-textured as dust.

He notices
the stark potential
of tarnished water

for the glass-plate photograph:
how there are slate tones
and oiliness together

and how, in standing pools
and running drains,
it coats the children's feet

with ubiquitous, gritty ink.
Alleyways and backyards
snag on his mind:

he can barely pass an entry
without assessing
the effect the diagonal

of a porterhouse roof
beside a streetlight
might produce, whereas

to photograph a yard
on Little York Street—
its ruin of toppled bricks

and broken guttering,
the windows of its houses,
open holes—

is to cast the viewer out
onto the no-man's-land
of her own estate

and to prove the eye is banked
as much by what unravels
as by flint.

There is the tidy shop
he makes his tidy living in
selling a wallet

of possible poses
for posterity: the Father
with his watch-chain,

the Sailor on his stool.
But for this commission
from the Corporation

he's sending home
dispatches from Sebastopol
Street in which

a man by the railings
ghosts himself
by turning his head too soon.

One cannot tell
if the room in the photograph
entitled *Number 36*

is inhabited—
light from the missing
upper storey is shafted

by jutting planks,
the fire-black walls
are crystalline

and yet outside similar terraces
with crumbling masonry
and dark for doors,

in bedraggled
unspeakable arcs
he's conjured with his shillings,

each child strong enough
to manage it
carries a child.

HOME BIRTH

The night your sister was born in the living room
you lay on your bed, upstairs, unwaking,
Cryptosporidium frothing and flourishing
through the ransacked terraces of your small intestine
so that, come morning, you, your bedding, me,
the midwife even, had to be stripped and washed.
Your father lifted you up like a torch
and carried you off to the hospital.

You came back days later, pale and feverish,
and visited us in the bedroom in your father's arms.
You turned your head to take her in: this black-haired,
tiny, yellow person who'd happened while you slept.
And you were the white dot of the television, vanishing—
vanishing—just before the screen goes dark.

A DAY'S BLINDNESS

December. The year at the back of it
blown and shrunk to dark
in the morning, dark in the afternoon
and the light in between
like the pale blue flicker of a pilot light
in a boiler's black intestine.

There was the usual breakfast
—coffee, soda bread, jam—
neither one of them speaking.
Her slept-on hair. The papers
still to go out for and a walk
to the top of the road and back,

past crows' nests fisted in trees,
to look at the Lough. It happened
at once: no jolt, no warning,
no shutter cranking low
over everything, no shadows
starting off on the periphery

like hares in fields
then gradually thickening.
He stood up to carry his plate and cup
to the sink and couldn't see.
He sat back down. The clocks
went on consuming Saturday.

He would have needed practice
at being blind to pretend to be sighted.
He had none, so she saw.
The son was away in Florida.
He asked her to leave, and for hours then,
as through the womb's wall,

he heard her about the house,
moving around upstairs,
using the bathroom, and perhaps
just once—or twice?—
saying something soft
and incoherent into the telephone.

Outside, at a quarter to four,
a watery sunset broke over
the squat hills. He couldn't tell
the lifting and the thud
of the returning dark apart.
He sat on at the table,

rolling crumbs beneath his thumbs
and waiting, either for what was taken
to be handed back—
the fridge, the kettle, his cuff-linked shirt—
or for the kleptomaniac visitor
he couldn't lock out

to be done with it, finally,
to sever the link—
to haul him up out of his chair,
into the hall, and through the brown door
to a garden ruined with hooves
and there would be

horses set loose from the Bond Yard
where his father worked
in the Hungry Thirties,
their coats engrained with soot
and their heads encased in steam,
accusing him.

Movement Is Life

—slogan of the Women's League of Health and Beauty, 1930–1939

Hyde Park, 1936. Cold enough for scarves and hats
among the general populace, but not for the fifteen thousand
    women
from the League of Health and Beauty performing callisthenics
on the grass. It could be snowing, and they of Bromley-Croydon,
    Slough,
Glasgow, Belfast, would don no more than a pair of satin knickers
and a sleeveless satin vest to spin and stretch and bow
the body beautiful. Athens in London, under a sodden sky,
and Winnie and Molly and Doris metamorphosed.

On the edge of the revolving staves of arms and legs,
pale as comfrey—an army not yet on the move but almost ready—
there are tents for scones and tea. Kiddies, brought to watch
in caps and plaits, wriggle on deckchairs. Their mothers
carry vast, forbidden handbags on their laps and smell
of Lily of the Valley. All around the periphery,
in huddled clumps of overcoats and smoke,
from offices and railway yards, men joke and talk, gesticulate—

but mostly they just look, quietly and sharply focused,
like eyeing up the horses at a racecourse, but with much more
     choice.
For those crammed in steaming picturehouses later, a commentator,
brusquely charmed, declares *the perfection of British womanhood:*
to them belongs the future!—while the ghost of Mary Bagot Stack,
whose dream this is, smiles back. Their hair cut short, slim,
co-ordinated as the League of German Maidens or a chorus set
from Hollywood, fit for birth, the women twirl and kick,

do foot-swings and scissor-jacks, link hands or fall
suddenly flat as pegs in a collapsible building, then bounce back
up again, for movement is life and they are keeping moving.
To hell with it, they may as well be saying. Twist.
To hell with Lizzie Evans and her bitching hate.
With blood and vinegar. With getting in the tin bath last.
With laddered stockings. With sore wrists at the factory.
I've got the fresh-air body they promised me. Twist. Its electricity.

FUR

At 25 and 29 respectively, Hans Holbein's
burly furred ambassadors haven't got long to go:
the pox, the plague, the ague, a splinter
in the finger, a scratch at the back of the throat
or an infection set into the shoulder joint
might carry them off, in a matter of writhing
hours, at any instant—

                    Too obvious a touch

to set the white skull straight.   Better
to paint it as something other: driftwood
up-ended by magic from the right-hand side
of the tesserae carpet; to let it hang
like an improbable boomerang just under
the clutch of pipes, the lute with the broken
string, still casting a shadow . . .

For there is bewitchery in those brown beards yet—
in the (slightly) rakish tilt to the saucer hat
of the ambassador on the left.

FOOL'S GOLD

For other men
the world is a woman
and their craving assuageable.
To say *every waking thought*
is surely to exaggerate,
but in my bowel

as much as in
my brain, my foremost sin
is gold. Its pristine glint and heft,
vaulted beneath my palace
in coins and necklaces,
masks, goblets,

was not enough
to stop the famished wolf
of my desire, to shut its throat.
So therefore, John Wright,
who stole and dipped
in your magic vat

a rose from my

buttonhole, smilingly,

and then lifted it out transmuted

into gold—you proffered

the key and did

not know it

to a blissful

plenitude, my soul's

ultimate, jubilant relief. I witnessed

tarnished candelabras

lowered as brass

come up licked

by the sun;

your workshop hung

with busts and angels, merchants' seals

and swords so luminescent

light itself sent

spies to steal

their secret.

And while chariots

and stallions and my own slick

mounted, radiant self bloomed

instantly in my mind,

I knew the trick

to set me there,

my newfound noble elixir,

the needle to be passed through,

the famed alchemical ingot

I could not do without—

was you.

The Royal children have been sent a gift—
A map of Europe from 1766
Complete with longitude, painted onto wood,
Like any other map in brown and green and red,
But then disfigured: cut up into parts,
A disassembly of tiny courts
Strewn across the table. There is a key
To help the children slot, country by country,
The known traversable world in place:
Little Tartary, Swedish Lapland, France,
The Government of Archangel. The sea
Has been divided into squares, crudely,
As though the cast-iron sides of nations
Still applied (but with more attention
To geometry) while the engraver's signature
—A circle, his name, a folded flower—
Has been deftly sawn in half. If successful,
The three young princes and the oldest girl
(This is not, after all, a lesson in diplomacy
So she can play too) will, ironically,
Undo the puzzle's title and its claim:
Europe Divided in Its Kingdoms
Shall be Europe reconfigured, whole.
They start in the top left corner with the scale

Then fill the other corners in: 'Part of Africa',
A scroll, the blank of simply 'Asia'
Rolling off to hordes and steppes and snow
Beyond the boundary. Outlines follow,
Aided by exquisite lettering:
'The Frozen Ocean' solidifies across the map's ceiling . . .
And so the Royal children spend an hour
Staring and exclaiming, clicking together
(What joy!) the angled buttress of a continent—
Their own unlikely island on a slant
By its farthest edge, and in their trance ignore
What will no longer fit: Aotearoa, America.

Vitya pledges his brigade of Pioneers will plant
half as many fruit trees as the other Pioneers.
Kiryusha pledges *his* brigade, the best of the detachment,
will match the trees of all brigades together, including Vitya's.
Their brigades work the last shift simultaneously.
The preceding brigades of the detachment
plant forty trees. Both pledges are fulfilled exactly.
How many trees does the whole detachment plant?

Answer: a kind of Latin, finished and intricate,
or a box of glass-plate negatives from 1887
unearthed by accident of Newcastle cloth market.
The Oceanic Whitetip Shark. Ectoplasm.
Natasha Ivanova on her collective farm
working out the most efficient way to harvest cotton.

And then he died.
And so I drove to where
he'd lived. I don't know why.
To stand across the street,
perhaps, hands in my pockets,
a happenstance observer

of the bricks, the Georgian
front, the chimney pots
and guttering, the bin,
the hedge, the fence,
appearing all-at-once
untenanted, bereft—

to take a photograph
or two of how that looked.
But his house was a smashed
hive, all industry and ruin:
the door was open;
vans with their backs

thrown wide cluttered
the driveway; men he never knew
in life were loading up
painting after painting—
portraits, landscapes, mill-scenes—
stripping every room

of his obsessions.
And so I intervened, crying theft
and history, and they listened.
And I was given half
an hour to photograph
what was left

before they finished.
Light inside the hallway,
even in February: without a flash
the staircase seeming flounced
in the train of a bridal dress,
shimmery

as the white space
in the foreyards of the factories
his buckled, blank-faced
people bent their bodies to.
The mantelpiece in the living room
strewn with stories—

postcards, knick-knacks,
impromptu napkin sketches;
the bar-talk of the clocks,
each set to a different time
in case their simultaneous chimes
distressed him; likenesses

of his parents scowling down.
But as though I stood in Lascaux
among its sprinting fawns
and my very breath
was wrecking what I stared at,
there were absences also:

squares of thin-lined stains
where, moments earlier,
pictures in their frames
had kept their residence—
impossible now to distinguish
which. My camera

clicked and whirled.
Upstairs I found his studio.
I changed the film.
They'd been in here
but not for long—everywhere,
archipelagos

of canvases he'd lain
against the window or the walls
still held their chains.
Persons, closer up than anything
of his I'd ever seen:
a boy and girl,

huddled and lovely
against a fogged-out background;
a man and his family,
everyone in it
round-shouldered and perplexed
by being found;

a child hitching a lift
in a barrow. And then the sea,
over and over: with a black ship
smoking into harbour,
or a distraction of yachts, or
waves and horizon only—

de-peopled, the tide
that one day didn't turn
but swallowed
the cacophony
of Salford and Pendlebury
and kept on coming on.

I had a minute
in the bedroom with Rossetti's
luscious women, standing silent
guard about his bed.
The counterpane re-made.
And then the foreman called me

from the first-floor landing—
they had to be getting on,
I should be going—and I had time
for a final shot
on my botched way out:
his trilby and his mac, hanging

from a hook, in black and white.

MIGRAINE

And it's happening yet again:
vandals set loose in the tapestry room
with pin-sharp knives. Such lovely scenes
as this day's scrubbed-white clouds
and shock of scarlet blooms
across the wasteground

looking abruptly damaged—
stabbed-through from the back
so that a dozen shining pin-sized
holes appear at random. Then widen.
Soon even the grass has been unpicked,
the gorse hacked open.

I can no longer see your face.
Posed in unravelling sleeves
and disappearing lace,
I have given up all hope for what was whole—
the monkey under the orange tree,
the tatterdemalion nightingale.

DAUGHTER

AFTER ROBERT PINSKY

I

She wakes at 7am—
her internal clock
unstintingly accurate—
and can sleep twelve hours
at a stretch without
losing hold of her last thought.
The grievance she fell
asleep with: *you didn't
get me rice milk* or
*you didn't sing me
song 'bout Tommy Thumb*—
her dawn declaration.
Though she'll also ask
is it morning?
just to check
she hasn't missed
the best and purest
portion of her day, the bit
with her brother and breakfast
in it, by being away.

The dresses and tops
in her wardrobe
smell of fabric conditioner—
sugar, vanilla, baking soda—
and are frequently washed.
The clothes she harries
off and leaves in heaps
on stairs and sofas
so she can flash
about the house
with nothing on—
a moon-pale, decelerating
balloon—recall whiskey:
layered, earthy, consisting
of neither sweat nor
excrement but of what
her deeper body's left
behind itself in warmth.
I cannot tell the strands
of it apart.

Cut off by the Atlantic,
half her family
are permanently absent
though she hasn't
noticed this yet.
Her world is still
the roof over 'safe'
in the Japanese pictograph.
Her fiercest, non-human
attachments are to
vibrantly coloured objects
—orange plate, red fork—
she cannot eat without.
She's learning this house
like a psalm: the crack
in the kitchen sink,
the drawers and all
their warring contents,
the geography of each room
immutable as television.

When visitors come
she's keen to show them
the most horrific thing
she knows: Rien Poortvliet's
picture of a Snotgurgle
in the *Bantam Book of Gnomes*.
Scabrous, radically
lopsided, huge—
he's forcing a gnome
through a mangle
while his sidekick
black rat laughs. The book
falls open at his face.
She might be Persephone,
bravely showing off
what she's survived,
but it's probably the snot
she's more delighted by:
the viscous, glittering rivulets
he hasn't wiped away.

v

In Timothy Leary's
eight-circuit system
of human evolution
there's a drug for every stage.
Acquiring language
or the Symbol State
(concerning itself with maps
and artefacts) is mimicked
by amphetamines:
crystal meth, Benzedrine.
Silent too long as an infant,
our daughter talks all day—
her toys, her toes,
her pictures, her minutely
attenuated hierarchy
of friends—
like a businessman
on the last train home
after one too many espressos,
selling you his dream.

A soldier returned from a war
was how my P6 spelling book put it: I saw

cripples with tin cans for coins
in dusty scarlet, back from some spat of Empire.

Later I became aware of buildings
built in squares around a courtyard

where every room looked down
to a fountain

rinsing and bleaching the light
assiduously as the women

who in folded hats like wings
washed clean their wounds.

My erstwhile stepfather was one
for whom Vietnam

was a constantly recurring dream—
the jungle inching its tendrils

into his lungs until he becomes
half-man, half-vine, asphyxiating.

The word itself has a click in it.
It halts before the ending.

Boats left stranded in trees.
The ones that survive are amphibian.

As I speak, there is something muscled
and bloody in the sink

the boy young enough to be my son
spat out and I can't look.

I don't know how he got inside my house.
The stereo is playing "Buckets of Rain"

by Dylan,
over and over again.

was *not like last winter*, we said, when winter
had ground its iron teeth in earnest: Belfast
colder than Moscow and a total lunar eclipse
hanging its Chinese lantern over the solstice.
Last winter we wore jackets into November
and lost our gloves, geraniums persisted,
our new pot-bellied stove sat unlit night
after night and inside our lungs and throats,
embedded in our cells, viruses churned out
relaxed, unkillable replicas of themselves
in the friendlier temperatures. Our son
went under. We'd lie awake, not touching,
and listen to him cough. He couldn't walk
for weakness in the morning. Thoracic,
the passages and hallways in our house
got stopped with what we would not say—
how, on our wedding day, we'd all-at-once
felt shy to be alone together, back
from the cacophony in my tiny, quiet flat
and surrounded by flowers.

A MATTER OF LIFE AND DEATH

On the afternoon I'm going into labour so haltingly it's still easy
    to bend and breathe, bend and breathe, each time the erratic clamp
        sets its grip about my pelvis, then releases—

I take a nap, eat lunch and while you pen a letter to our impending
    offspring
    explaining who we are, what there is on offer in the house
        we don't yet know we'll leave, to be handed over

on his eighteenth birthday like a key to the demesne, sit front-to-back
    on an upright chair in the living room and switch on the television.
        World War II. David Niven is faltering after a bombing op

in a shot-up plane. *Conservative by nature, Labour by conviction,*
    he quotes Sir Walter Raleigh: *O give me my scallopshell of quiet,*
        my staff of faith to walk upon, while a terrified American radio girl

listens in. It's all fire and ravenous engine noise—he can't land
    because the fuselage is damaged and he hasn't a parachute.
        Then, because he'd *rather fall than fry,* he bails out anyway—

a blip on the screen vanishing into cloud cover. The girl hides her
    face in her hands.
    The baby drops a fraction of an inch and the next contraction hurts.
        I know I'm at the gentlest end of an attenuated scale

of pain relief: climbing the stairs, a bath, two aspirin, tapering down
    as the hours
        roll on (and we relocate to hospital) to gas and air, pethidine,
            a needle in the spine, and go out to walk the sunny verges

of our cul-de-sac like a wind-up, fat-man toy, tottering every five
    minutes or so
        into a bow. Nobody's home. The bins are still out on the road
            after this morning's pick-up. The light is slant and filled

with running gold. Back inside, the film has switched to Technicolor
    monochrome: an anachronistic afterlife in grey in which dead
        airmen
            sign in under 'name' and 'rank', the Yanks smack gum

and swagger, *isn't this swell?* and a legion of otherworldly women
    with hair rolled high as dunes hand out enormous plaster wings
        to the just-deceased. The dead are invoiced for,

like battleships or teapots, their names on the list ticked off
    as they swing through each allotted doorway clean and whole
        and orderly—the incomprehensible machinery of life and death

a question of books that balance. And there's this sudden tug inside,
    rigging straining taut and singing, and I cry out for the first time,
        and in you come to coax and soothe as though I'm doing
            something—

running a marathon, climbing a mountain—instead of being forced
    back down
        into my seat by some psychopathic schoolmarm over and over again,
            stay. And I think of my granny and her *forty-six hours*

of agony, shifting my mother from one world to the next, and how
    that birth
        cut short her happiness at the Raleigh bicycle factory in Nottingham
            where her youth was spent in *secret war work*, typing up invoices.

Back in heaven, there's about as much commotion as there's been
    in a million
        years (a slight shake of the head by the woman in charge, a sigh)
            because David Niven, who should have arrived but hasn't,

landed on a beach and—how?—survived, met the American radio
    operator
        as she cycled home after the night-shift, and fell in love. He must
        be sent for.
            Down below, they're already looking post-coital: picnicking
                in civvies

on a homespun Tartan rug in a Technicolor rose garden. I'm not
    supposed
        to show up at the hospital for hours, or not until the cervix
            has done its slow, industrial cranking-wide enough to be marked

by a thumb-span, and the problem is I don't know what that
    means, or how to tell,

or how much worse the pain is going to get (answer: a lot)
        and so the afternoon grows hot and narrow and you abandon

your confessions altogether and the botched clock of paradise with
    seven hands
    across its face ticks on the wall. *I've seen it many times,* said my
        granny,
        when a new life comes into a family, an old life goes out—

as though there were checks and balances, birth weighted against
    death
    like a tidy invoice, and a precise amount of room allotted the
        living.
        Before we inch upstairs to the bathroom to test what sweet
            relief

is granted, after all, by a bath and lavender oil, I catch sight
    of a magical marble escalator—the original stairway to heaven—
        with David Niven
        captive on its steps being hauled away to the sound of a
            clanking bell

from his radiant girlfriend, and I imagine my granny, who died
   three weeks ago
   on a hospital ward in Chesterfield, *making room* as she herself
      predicted,
      not dumb and stricken and hollowed out with cancer

but young, glamorous, childless, free, in her 1940s' shoes and sticky
   lipstick,
   clicking about the office of new arrivals as though she owns it,
      flicking open the leather-bound ledger and asking him to sign.

SIGNATURES

Belfaste is a place meet for a corporate town, armed

with all commodities, as a principal haven, wood

and good ground, standing also upon a border . . .

—extract from a letter to the Privy Council

from the Earl of Essex, 1573

I

Where nothing was, then something. Six months ago
most of this was sludge and a gangrenous slip-way
dipping its ruined foot in the sea—a single rusted gantry
marking the spot where a small town's population
of Protestant men built a ship the size of the Empire State Building.
Smashed cars and wreckers' yards flourished in between.

II

A skin-stripping wind. This morning I walk on concrete
smooth as a runway with a full-scale outline laid in light
of the uppermost deck. Railings as over a stern.
Grass. Seating. The memorial for the dead hosts names
I can't pronounce—*Sjöstedt, Taussig, Backström*—
in immaculate glass. Once, I count a surname seven times.

THROUGH THE EYE OF A NEEDLE

Still shorter than my hip
but solid, heavy as a scooped-full
coal-scuttle, hair so fingerwrapped and knotted
it stands in coils about her ears and won't comb flat,
cherubic, with that dimpled roll of fat above the buttocks
the stubby painted angels carry brightly, her feet and hands a fan
she opens frequently to admire the slotted hinges of her bones,
to blow between the gaps, arm-skin like powder down,
an almost-constant frown atop a round bright box
with treasure in it: seamless lips, even teeth,
eyes that loop the swallows up

on their traceable tethers
to harry them, upside-down, into
the huge room of her brain and make them fit
the vivid, random furniture pre-assembled there—
buttercup petals crushed on her palm, the Teapot Song,
dust motes and the taste of rust, shadows under her cot that grow
vast without a night-light, hunger, always satisfied,
its own fat child in a caul and sleepiness a wall
you dig-a-hole-and-curl-up under—
where they leave their threaded
flight-path like the imprint
on a carpet of a stain.

THE DOCTORS

blurt it out like a Polaroid

—Paul Muldoon

In this country
they are desecrating photographs—
those that tell the truth of their own flown moment
simply as it was, that are naïve as schoolchildren
set down in a bewildering classroom and bid to speak
their name and place of birth in a foreign tongue,
who revert, instinctively, to their own, as slates
and straps and canes rain down upon them.

It is the camera's
inherent generosity of outlook
which is more often than not at fault:
the one-whose-name-we-dare-not-whisper
sitting at breakfast with Our Great Leader
on holiday in the Urals, or idly grinding his teeth
in a dim committee room, his glasses like miniature
headlights reflecting the flash.

With scissors,

nail files, ink and sellotape, he has been vanished—

alongside other party operatives who touched

His sleeve, or didn't clap for long enough, or loved

their wives, or laughed, or who pointed the way

down some rickety steps as though He needed help

—whole politburos cropped to a man, or at most

a handful of survivors ranged around a chess table,

scratched absences

over their shoulders made luminous as moons.

It is addictive: the urge to utter a language

both singular and clean. It is progressive—

how the power to transform a conspirator into a pillar

transmutes, in turn, to the eradication

of the accidental as a class of photograph:

how litter, bleak weather, a sneer,

or too many smiling

parents who later disappeared are also doctored.

And should anyone be missed—turning up

in textbooks before the grave extent

of their transgression's been established—

a nation's girls and boys, all trained

in proper parlance, their fingers stained with soot,

draw over women's faces black balloons.

In woods and lakes, car boots, freezers, huts,
in ministers' apartments where their flailing last

went on too long, garrotted, poisoned, hanged
or sliced in half and lain like Solomon's child

on the bridge of a border between two countries—
the myriad murdered dead of Scandinavia

are seeping their slow corrosion into the air, into
the tap water, and must be found. So many crimes

unsolved you'd think those dressed-down cops
in their open-plan offices balanced books

on their heads all day or practised on the sly
for the Eurovision Song Contest. But wait—

Denmark and Sweden's cleverest women
are on their way: obsessed, lonely, semi-autistic

and wired as no man with them ever is
to sense, without exactly evidence, where corpses

have been left: plastered into a crevice in a flat
in an affluent suburb or strung amongst the cables

of a lift-shaft in a disused meat-packing plant.
F# Minor, writes Johann Mattheson in 1713,

is *abandoned, singular, misanthropic,* and *leads
to great distress. We cannot well accompany*

the Devil in any other key. It will invert anything—
"Jingle Bells," "Home on the Range," Dick Van Dyke's

"Chim Chim Cher-ee"—turning them hopeless
and ironic, just as glass-walled houses

in the forest, immaculate kitchens, flat-pack rooms
sprung wide and nifty public transport systems

translate to mist in the brightly lit underground
hall of the coroner's workspace where three

blonde girls from the badminton squad
have hit their brutal terminus. We are given

less than a second
with their lacerated legs and hands.

Then cut to the churning sea with the moon on it—
the music making it worse—then nothing.

YARD POEM

FOR PAUL MADDERN

The rat on your salvaged pallet out the back
among pots, bricks, paperweights,
bees made of glass, a litter
of pink petals from the balsawood trellis,
the blown-open tongues of the honeysuckle—
is already a nest for flies and getting rained on.
It shifts its weight every fifteen minutes or so
so we know it's still living.

With bodies as blue as a peacock's waistcoat
or coal's first concession to fire,
the flies shimmer at intervals
along the animal's flank: so still
you'd think they'd died together.
Now neither sex, nor leaf-sweep, nor thunder
can cleave them. The eyes of the rat are sealed tight
as though pencilled shut with eyeliner.

More flies alight. It rains harder. I can't look.
The rat draws its consciousness
back into its own scuttled bone-shack.
And the blue of the flies shines, jewelled,
unfazable, a mineral attack
on the walls of our final kingdom—
burglars, with a sense of grievance,
desecrating the Hall of Ishtar.

My son's awake at ten, stretched out along
his bunk beneath the ceiling, wired and watchful.
The end of August. Already the high-flung
daylight sky of our Northern solstice dulls
earlier and earlier to a clouded bowl;
his Star of David lamp and plastic moon
have turned the dusk to dark outside his room.

Across the Lough, where ferries venture blithely
and once a cruise ship, massive as a palace,
inched its brilliant decks to open sea—
a lighthouse starts its own nightlong address
in fractured signalling; it blinks and bats
the swingball of its beam, then stands to catch,
then hurls it out again beyond its parallax.

He counts each creamy loop inside his head,
each well-black interval, and thinks it just for him—
this gesture from a world that can't be entered:
the two of them partly curtained, partly seen,
upheld in a sort of boy-talk conversation
no one else can hear. That private place, it answers,
with birds and slatted windows—I've been there.

THE COAL JETTY

Twice a day,
    whether I'm lucky enough
        to catch it or not,

the sea slides out
    as far as it can go
        and the shore coughs up

its crockery: rocks,
    mussel banks, beach glass,
        the horizontal chimney stacks

of sewer pipes,
    crab shells, bike spokes.
        As though a floating house

fell out of the clouds
    as it passed
        the city limits,

Belfast bricks, the kind
    that also built the factories
        and the gasworks,

litter the beach.
    Most of the landing jetty
        for coal's been washed

away by storms; what stands—
    a section of platform
        with sky on either side—

is home now to guillemots
    and cormorants
        who call up

the ghosts of nineteenth-
    century hauliers
        with their blackened

beaks and wings.
    At the lowest ebb,
        even the scum at the rim

of the waves
    can't reach it.
        We've been down here

before, after dinner,
    picking our way
        over mudflats and jellyfish

to the five spiked
hallways underneath,
spanned like a viaduct.

There's the stink
of rust and salt,
of cooped-up

water just released
to its wider element.
What's left is dark and quiet—

barnacles, bladderwrack,
brick—but book-ended
by light,

as when Dorothy
opens her dull
cabin door

and what happens outside is Technicolor.

Dewey is going fishing with his father to the swamp.
The earth is powder-dry. The sky is laden.
The river's a half-drained basin with the bottom poking through:
mud, tree-stumps, driftwood spiked like antlers, rocks.
They have a pole each slung over one shoulder
and a bucket for the catch. There are no fish.

Miss Hattie Purcell from the post office is making it rain.
She surprises them, sitting in the puddle of her clothes,
concentrating. Of everyone back at the Royals—
the schoolmaster, the Seed & Feed owner—
only she has the power. They go round her
like skirting a preacher they haven't the time for.

The indigo bushes are latticed with climbing vines.
Violets are blooming, and frowsy white flowers
Dewey doesn't know the name of that happen in spring.
They run a rickety plank to a smashed-up bridge
in the middle of the Little Muscadine
and drop their baited lines. Schtum as a heron,

Miss Hattie sits rigid on the crest of the riverbank,
whatever language magic might be made of
running in her mind. *Blackie!* Then again, *Blackie!*
And here comes his father's name, shot across
to them out of the maples. *Blackie!* Miss Hattie
doesn't move. Some other lady entirely

has gone and placed her round bright face in the branches
where a circle of sun has landed and uttered this cry.
Then she runs away. The swamp is still as a Sunday.
She must be about to die, thinks Dewey,
watching for his fish. His father flourishes
a lunch from his overall pockets and they laugh.

It starts to rain—yes, praise to heaven rising
where it falls O hallelujahs—one plopped drop at a time.
Soon the river's so ploughed and puckered
it looks like a muddy field you'd step onto and be safe.
And if the rain could be translated into words
Little You and Little Me, Little You and Little Me

would be the closest thing to meaning you could catch.

Double Trouble, The Ghost Café, Late at Night
in the Bedroom: each Mutoscope tells its story
to whoever steps right up, drops a penny in its slot

and cranks the handle. Mimicking decency,
the poster shows a solid Victorian gentlewoman
stooping to its glass as though sniffing narcissi

in a window box, her hat a fountain.
A World of Moving Pictures, Very Popular
in Public Places, it is, in fact, an intimate machine

whose jittery flickerings of marital war,
a monkey on a bicycle, or a lady being undressed
from a through-the-keyhole, what-the-butler-saw

perspective, no one else can watch
at the same time. Sir or Madam, yours is the hand
that squares the frame, undoes the catch

at the top of the reel and sets eight hundred
separate photographs tumbling into blackness
against a brown-paper background

but showing you each shot before they vanish.
Only for you do the two mute girls on stage
who falter at first, erratic as static

in the synaptic gap between each image,
imperceptibly jolt to life—
grinning, tap-dancing, morphing into footage,

their arms like immaculate pistons, their legs like knives . . .
It lasts a minute, their having-been-written onto light.

THE HOUSE OF OSIRIS
IN THE FIELD OF REEDS

I'm turning forty. Not on my birthday
(still, as I write, six weeks away) but over months.
It's like a migraine: that sludgy disconnectedness
starting in the brain, hours before the hammering.
I've forgotten my name and my husband's name
in the run-up to the full-scale meltdown.

All through last winter, each day
made to bear the pressure of impending loss.
Soon it will no longer be like this. The lean girls
picnicking in the park, their haul of charity-shop
dresses at their feet, listening to the Smiths,
have long since picked themselves up and vanished

down the tall-grass corridor of rooks and smoke.
I can no longer remember their faces, or what
the sky over Dublin inscribed on my skin
the year I'd just left home, or even the impact
of first-time, proper sex, of being unwrapped.
But turning forty banishes my younger self

to a separate outhouse, somewhere stony
and impassable, hot, fly-infested, like the city
of Tetu on the Nile, which became the Otherworld
for all of Egypt, and I cannot get across.
Death was so much closer then, of course—
I'd be dead already or at least a grandmother;

if rich, I'd have my orders pre-prepared
for the sarcophagus maker, the Shabti carver,
the weaver of the shroud; I'd have selected
the spells for my coffin-lid, the amulets required
to survive the guarded entrances of the afterlife,
the tricky test with hearts and feathers.

O exiled one, so you may escape the heat
and torpor of that barren place, and pass instead
to the Field of Reeds, and do no work there,
discover by your grave cloths a replica of yourself
in turquoise faience, fashioned with a basket.
Here, it says. I'll do it. Take me.

Ingrid in her shawl's been here since nine,
burdening the tables on loan
from the church downstairs with Babushka dolls
and caviar, handkerchiefs and wine

from Yugoslavia, Bulgarian perfume.
My brother and I ask for a job
and are handed pink-and-white posters
of *Peace & Détente* to decorate the room.

It's trickier than we thought
to stick them straight so secretly we give up.
Almost everyone's smoking.
In the background, "Kalinka" on cassette

belted out by the Red Army Choir
wobbles towards its peak. There's tea,
coffee, Irish stew, and a cool display
of anti–Mrs Thatcher paraphernalia—

pens in the shape of nails for her coffin
we'll buy and use in school.
Shop stewards come, and sympathisers
who, once a year, like Christians,

demonstrate their faith, the odd
bewildered lured-in shopper looking for soap,
or socks, but mostly it's just us:
Card Carriers and the Kids Thereof,

filling up the air with fevered talk. By four,
Rosemary Street's ablaze in the solstice dark.
We pack what's left of the wooden trains and vodka
into crates for another year and repair

to the Duke of York, where once
an *actual* Soviet Representative—tall, thin—
in frost-inflected English gave a speech,
and I clutched my lemonade and was convinced.

Honey,

You've requested a Raymond Chandler spin-off,
a spoof in style, but from the blonde's perspective:
let's say the secretary in the one about the coin
called a *Brasher Doubloon*, gone missing
from a Pasadena mansion. We're in this thing together:
busier than a PI who never simply talks but utters
wisecracks like a jeweller stringing pearls;
happier too, more stranded in domestic detail,
but, hell, tonight I've drawn the blinds, clicked on
the tasselled lamp, unplugged the telephone,
set out two highballs, and before the children cry
upstairs, pulled you down beside me by your tie.
So I say, it's like this. Some guy walks into the office
with an unlit cigarette, wearing 'unimpressed'
like a drape-cut jacket, and looks her over.
He looks everything over—plants, ashtrays, furniture—
with a languid, expert eye, the type of man who gives
a girl offence by offering advice about her gloves
or hair or make-up uninvited. He knows too much,
about guns and broads and books and chess,
the likelier scenarios, which kinda hurts his soul
and which kinda makes him smooth and cool and powerful.

Our glasses clink. Then you say, a-okay,
but what's with her? And I don't know. Witchery
in the garden room for sure—towering flaxes
pressed against the pane, an alcoholic mistress
and a life so narrow, probably from the outset,
its pathetic little batch of dull effects
could fit inside one suitcase. Which is not her fault.
And you know what? Maybe hair pulled taut
against her head and a simple linen dress
(so weird he notes it twice) is just her choice.
The whiskey seeps its spiced and easy heat
along our spines, the house is oddly quiet,
and I'm suddenly adrift in how the road
to Idle Valley dips and curves towards
its secret: a thousand lighted windows
on the hill, a moon so sharp its shadows
look cut out with an engraving tool,
and Marlowe in his car, escaping the patrol . . .

Now kiss me.

Dull summer.
A field of standing corn
we can't imagine ever ripening
and a tunnel of trees so thick we half-expect
Narnia at the end of it—
a halter

of flyblown ivy
round every trunk. A bridge
disappearing in lime-green foliage
arches overhead, a blocked road mouths its dark,
and then the car park,
still empty

except for us
and an ostentation
of peacocks, standing to attention
in front of the toilet-block, whose women have vanished.
Their yowling is anguished,
like coitus

without relief,
and bespeaks just such a place
as this, with crumbling walls and trellises
but with gods at its centre, off-white statuary,
visible heat. It automatically
rehearses grief.

A boy who wants
to be king raises his aquamarine
fan. His throat and belly are shining
through the hanging twilight in the middle of the day.
Then, aggrieved, he turns away
as punishment

on our daughter
who has gone and brought
waving hands and shrieking to his court
so thoughtlessly. His underfeathers ripple like gauze
in a waterfall, outlawing
us from colour.

Inside a moss-
covered Nissen hut left over
from the war, the aristocratic owners
of this once-estate have fed, bred, cocooned, released
thirty-eight species
of moth

and butterfly
~~to hang out their wings~~
like washing on the heads of jasmine,
split oranges, nectarines, apple-halves, dish-scourers
soaking in honeywater
and on the eyes

of the hip-cocked
Cupid with a fountain at his feet.
She stands a second in diminished light,
her hair burnished and unruly, her mouth ajar, unsure
of the suddenly tropical air
that feels dropped

from heaven
and its fluttering tenants.
The heat pipes whine, fall silent.
The butterflies lift and settle indiscriminately
and could be unbearably heavy
or knock her down

for all she knows,
like her view of the sea
and its encroaching tides as wholly
unpredictable, as able to swallow the length and breadth
of the beach in a single breath.
Then off she goes,

an injured spouse
fixated on escape, unenthralled
by the swallowtails and the admirals,
back through the hanging shredded plastic curtain
that keeps the insects safe, to a garden
with a playhouse

and a climbing-frame,
where all her wishing terminates.
We finish our visit taking tea and cake
in her make-believe kitchen, obeying her commands,
wiping our mouths on our hands,
calling her name.

A LIE

That their days were not like our days,
the different people who lived in sepia—

more buttoned, colder, with slower wheels,
shut off, sunk back in the unwakeable house

for all we call and knock. And even the man
with the box and the flaming torch

who made his servants stand so still
their faces itched can't offer us what it cost

to watch the foreyard being lost
to cream and shadow, the pierced sky

placed in a frame. Irises under the windowsill
were the colour of Ancient Rome.

BLOG

I don't have girlfriends but I do have sex
with a different woman about three times a month.
Sometimes more. Sometimes less. I rarely ask.

They'll stop to talk to me in the supermarket
or on the bus. Off-handedly at first.
They're not made-up or drunk. We don't flirt

or analyse it. There's this tiny electrical thrill
gets passed like an egg-yolk slipping
between the cups of its own split shell.

They take me home. It happens. I leave. Simple.
They don't invite me to dinner or text.
It's easy and clean and consensual.

Then it happens again. Loneliness's overblown—
unless I'm just one of the unnaturally blessed.
My good friend Jack told me to write this down.

NOTES ON *Parallax and Selected Poems*

'FLIGHT'

I am indebted here to Michael McKeon's *The Origins of the English Novel, 1600–1740* (Baltimore, London: Johns Hopkins University Press, 1987), which first brought the 'miraculous' flight of Charles II in 1651 to my attention. Other details in the poem are taken from Samuel Pepys's *His Majesty Preserved: An Account of King Charles II's Escape After the Battle of Worcester*, first published in 1680 (London: Falcon Press, 1954).

'THE STATE OF THE PRISONS'

Two biographies of John Howard were crucial to the writing of this poem: Leona Baumgartner's *John Howard: Hospital and Prison Reformer* (Baltimore: John Hopkins University Press, 1939), and Martin Southwood's *John Howard: Prison Reformer* (London: Independent Press, 1958). The title of the poem comes from Howard's own publication, *The State of the Prisons*, first published in 1777.

'VANITY FAIR'

This poem is inspired by William Makepeace Thackeray's novel *Vanity Fair* (1847–1848), in which the widow Amelia Osborne (née Sedley) writes a letter to her long-term admirer, William Dobbin, after he has finally despaired of winning her love and left her. The consequence of this letter is that Dobbin returns to Amelia and they are married. Because the contents of the letter are not described by Thackeray, I have attempted to fill in what Thackeray left out.

'YORK'

This is a found poem based on the York Mystery Plays, in which the various guilds of the city were each responsible for writing and performing a play in the cycle. 'And episodes in between with a yet more fabulous cohabiting', and the two final lines, are my own.

'1801'

This is inspired by Dorothy Wordsworth's *The Grasmere Journals, 1800–1803* (Oxford: Oxford University Press, 1991).

'FOOL'S GOLD'

Here I imagine Prince Albert addressing John Wright, an English surgeon and inventor, in his electroplating workshop in Birmingham in 1840. The poem is inspired by the episode 'Gold' in the series *A History of Art in Three Colours*, written and presented by James Fox, and first broadcast on BBC Four in July 2012.

'PUZZLE'

This poem is inspired by Boris A. Kordemsky's *The Moscow Puzzles: 359 Mathematical Recreations* (Harmondsworth: Penguin, 1972).

'PHOTOGRAPHING LOWRY'S HOUSE'

I imagine the speaker of this poem to be Denis Thorpe, a photographer for *The Guardian*, who took photographs of the interior of L. S. Lowry's house just after the painter had died.

'A MATTER OF LIFE AND DEATH'

This poem draws heavily on the British film of the same title by Michael Powell and Emeric Pressburger, released in the United States as *Stairway to Heaven* (1946).

'THE DOCTORS'

This poem is inspired by David King's *The Commissar Vanishes* (New York: Metropolitan Books, 1997)—a study of how photographs were systematically falsified in Soviet-era Russia.

ACKNOWLEDGEMENTS

My sincere thanks to Michael Schmidt and the team at Carcanet Press for their work on my previous collections.

Thanks are due to the editors of the following publications in which some of these poems, or versions of them, have previously appeared: *An Anthology of Modern Irish Poetry* (Belknap Press of Harvard University Press, 2010), *The Antioch Review, Archipelago, Atlanta Review, Being Alive* (Bloodaxe Books, 2004), *The Cincinnati Review, Edinburgh Review, English Studies: A Journal of English Language and Literature, A Fine Statement* (Poolbeg Press, 2008), *The Guardian, The Independent on Sunday, Irish Pages, Jubilee Lines* (Faber & Faber, 2012), *Love Poet, Carpenter: Michael Longley at Seventy* (Enitharmon Press, 2010), *Metre, A Modern Don Juan* (Five Leaves Publications, 2014), *Modern Women Poets* (Bloodaxe Books, 2005), *The Moth, New Hibernia Review, The New Irish Poets* (Bloodaxe Books, 2004), *New Poetries II* (Carcanet Press, 1999), *New Walk, The Penguin Book of Irish Poetry* (Penguin Classics, 2010), *PN Review, Poetry Daily, Poetry Ireland Review, Poetry London, The Poetry Review, The SHOp, The Stinging Fly, Tongue: A Journal of Writing & Art, The Wake Forest Book of Irish Women's Poetry* (Wake Forest University Press, 2011), *The Wake Forest Series of Irish Poetry, Volume I* (Wake Forest University Press, 2004), and *The Yellow Nib*.

Thanks are due to the British Council for a seat on the Writers' Train across China in 2003, and for many other international trips and residencies.

I gratefully acknowledge the receipt of a Lannan Literary Fellowship in November 2007. Thanks are due to the Arts Council of Northern Ireland and the Heritage Lottery Fund (UK) for a Major Individual Artist Award in 2012.

Sinéad Morrissey was born in 1972 and grew up in Belfast,
Northern Ireland. She is the author of five poetry collections:
*There Was Fire in Vancouver, Between Here and There, The State
of the Prisons, Through the Square Window,* and *Parallax.*
Her awards include the Patrick Kavanagh Poetry Award,
an Eric Gregory Award, the Rupert and Eithne Strong
Award, the Michael Hartnett Poetry Award, first place in the
UK National Poetry Competition and, in 2007, a Lannan
Literary Fellowship. *Through the Square Window* and *Parallax*
were both recipients of the Irish Times Poetry Now Award for
best collection. In 2013, *Parallax* was awarded the T. S. Eliot
Prize. She teaches creative writing at the Seamus Heaney
Centre for Poetry, Queen's University, Belfast, and in
2013 was appointed Belfast's inaugural poet laureate.

Printed in the USA
CPSIA information can be obtained
at www.ICGtesting.com
LVHW091142150724
785511LV00005B/494

9 780374 536138